BITCOIN INVESTING FOR BEGINNERS

A BEGINNER'S GUIDE TO THE
CRYPTOCURRENCY WHICH IS CHANGING THE
WORLD. MAKE MONEY WITH
CRYPTOCURRENCIES, MASTER TRADING AND
UNDERSTAND BLOCKCHAIN CONCEPTS

SEBASTIAN ANDRES

SA PUBLISHING

CONTENTS

Introduction   v

Preface   ix

IMPORTANT NOTE   xi

1. THE HARD TRUTH ABOUT BITCOIN AND   1
   CRYPTOCURRENCIES
   LET'S START WITH THE BEGINNING, WHAT ARE   2
   CRYPTOCURRENCIES?

2. UNDERSTANDING BLOCKCHAIN AND BITCOIN   10
   TRANSACTIONS

3. BITCOIN FOR BEGINNERS, WHERE DO I START?   15
   HOW CAN YOU KEEP YOUR ACCOUNT SECURE?   19
   Where does the scam really occur?   28

4. WHERE CAN I BUY BITCOIN?   29
   Remember that Bitcoin never sleeps: 37
   Get organized: 37
   Control everything you invest: 37
   Don't wait too long: 38

5. WHERE TO STORE YOUR BITCOINS THE   39
   SAFEST WAY?
   The wonderful new world of marketplace 2.0   40
   HARD WALLETS the best way to securely and   44
   reliably store your Cryptocurrencies
   Trezor   45
   Ledger nano S   46
   Cover your back   48

6. HOW TO GET BITCOINS FOR FREE   50
   Want to get Bitcoins but don't have the money to buy   50
   them? Don't worry, this chapter is for you.
   Mining Bitcoins   51
   Have fun on sites that pay you with Bitcoin   53

7. BITCOIN TRADING   61

8. BITCOIN MINING WHAT IS IT ALL ABOUT?   70

9. ALTCOINS AND WHICH ONES CAN MAKE YOU   75
   WEALTHY
10. WHY SHOULD YOU START NOW?   83
11. MAKING PASSIVE INCOME WITH BITCOIN   90

   About the author   93

INTRODUCTION

Welcome

First of all, I would like to thank you for your trust and for choosing me as your guide to embark on this journey into the world of Cryptocurrencies. This book will help you to master this world and to obtain an excellent financial education through the comprehension and understanding of Cryptocurrencies, in short, we will go from the most basic to the most advanced.

We are aware that entering the world of Cryptocurrencies can be tedious and very slow, generally the pioneers in this type of technology are people who have no problem to generate passive income online. That's right, you can actually change your life in a 180-degree turn, as you will see later with some success stories in the following chapters.

This technology is here to stay and to give us, ordinary people, more freedom in the economic and financial field.

One of the things that caught my attention when I started to get interested in Cryptocurrencies back in 2011 was the concept of freedom that is related to currencies like Bitcoin, Monero, Dash, Zcash, etc. where the control of the whole process is always in the hand of the user and therefore the privacy they give us In this book I will teach you the different approaches to Cryptocurrencies and the technology behind: the Blockchain, because it works, what is the secret behind and also we will demolish some myths related to some concepts.

The goal of this book is to teach you to have a more complete and complex notion about Cryptocurrencies, from the most basic concepts such as knowing how everything works, how the pieces fit together to the most advanced where you will see and know which are the Cryptocurrencies that promise to increase their value in 2021 and 2022 so you can get some good profits (in the last chapters I share some that promise a lot).

I've also taken the time to recommend some resources to get you started on the right foot.

My goal, too, is not only to educate you but to motivate you too, to take that step that is so hard for you and take action, this is why I want to ask you one thing, do not give up throughout this book, follow my advice to the letter, I promise that by finishing this book and applying step by step my advice and teachings you will achieve a better understanding of this little world and according to your personal actions achieve financial freedom or also support this initiative that gives power to us citizens against the current financial system that is too manipulated and makes a few people rich.

Without further ado, let's get started!

Thank you very much for purchasing this book, I hope you enjoy it as much as I enjoyed writing it.

PREFACE

My Story

My name is SEBASTIAN ANDRES, I am an entrepreneur, writer, fitness enthusiast, healthy living, music and world traveler. Cryptocurrency enthusiast since 2011 when I started to get interested in this world. If I were to be honest, I feel extremely blessed by the life I got to live in this world and with the technologies we have today.

For more than 10 years I have focused on developing several internet businesses, which taught me to develop my own strategies and methods to generate passive income. Cryptocurrencies was one of them and that is how I achieved financial freedom.

The purpose of my books, which deal with business and self-help topics, is mainly to be a source of inspiration in order to generate a change in those who are not satisfied with the established and know that they can give more, that they can generate a positive change in their lives and get to design that lifestyle they want so much, and even achieve the longed-for financial freedom by taking ACTION and leaving aside the motivational and philosophical speeches that do not allow you to advance in your goals.

I hope my books will help you to give you that push that will propel you to help you achieve and accomplish your goals in life and business.

Enough Motivation, it's time to take action!

IMPORTANT NOTE

Something to keep in mind

Investing in financial markets such as Cryptocurrencies and other assets can lead to money losses. The purpose of this book is educational only and does not represent an investment recommendation.

Proceed with caution and at your own risk and remember, never invest more than you are willing to lose.

By continuing to read this book you accept this Warning.
Without further ado, let's continue.

1

THE HARD TRUTH ABOUT BITCOIN
AND CRYPTOCURRENCIES

Bitcoin is perhaps the most talked about cryptocurrency these days, everyone is talking about it. However, very few people really know what it is and that is where it makes a big difference. There are more and more people interested in having it because its value has skyrocketed in ways unthinkable a few years ago, reaching almost $70,000 dollars (in 2021). It can be said then that whoever owned a few Bitcoins bought in 2010 and sold them at their historical maximum in 2021, already has his life solved, and not only his own but also that of future generations since many managed to become millionaires thanks to this cryptocurrency.

The paradoxical thing about Bitcoin is precisely the fact that it is so famous and yet there are millions and millions of people who do not have the slightest idea what it is all about. In this book we will expose you to all the details, everything you need to know to really learn about Bitcoin so you can even enter the wonderful world of crypto assets and who knows, maybe achieve the financial freedom you long for.

We know it sounds complicated, we know that many of the terms associated with Bitcoin are complex and way ahead of their time, because most of them deal with a whole computer terminology that only geeks seem to understand. But don't be overwhelmed, we have great news for you. The first is that you don't need to be an expert to understand about Bitcoin because that's why you bought this book, you are in good hands, and the second is that if you get into the wonderful world of Cryptocurrencies, you can earn a lot of money, but a lot of money really, amounts that surely at this moment you could not even imagine.

But be careful, in this book we will not try to deceive you by telling you that everything happens quickly and overnight, no, that's not how it works. Only those who learn the nature of Cryptocurrencies can really take advantage of it, so let's start at the beginning so you can become a true connoisseur and you can really become an expert.

LET'S START WITH THE BEGINNING, WHAT ARE CRYPTOCURRENCIES?

Let's take the first step in this topic, Cryptocurrencies are virtual currencies with which you can pay for both goods and services virtually, that is, through electronic transactions. In other words, to make it even simpler: Cryptocurrencies are the money of the future, of the new era. Thanks to cryptocurrencies, cash will no longer be necessary; now you will be able to pay for anything, from goods to work done by professionals, all through virtual currencies, which are the famous cryptocurrencies. In short, we are facing what could be considered the future of money as we know it today. Just as many years ago goods were exchanged and it was decided to use currency, then banknotes and then plastic cards called credit cards, the most logical evolution goes hand in hand with Cryptocurrencies and they are here to stay.

WE KNOW that although Cryptocurrencies are a boom worldwide, there are still many places where people have no idea that they even exist, much less know what they are or how to use them. While in

China, Japan and the United States, just to mention three countries, several Cryptocurrencies have already been established in the market and people are already paying and getting paid through them. There are also places like Africa and Latin America where more than half of the population has never used them and most of them don't even know about them.

That maybe is your case, maybe like most people, you have heard about Cryptocurrencies but you have no idea what they are all about. Well, that is why it is important to know a bit of history and understand their origin.

The first known cryptocurrency started operating almost a decade ago, back in 2009, and since then it has been known as Bitcoin. Surely you have heard of it because today it is the most valuable, its value has soared to almost unimaginable levels, but when it was born, when it was just beginning to appear on the market, it was so cheap that by completing a couple of tasks on the internet you could earn a Bitcoin, in fact when it was formally released in August 2010, 1 Bitcoin (BTC) was worth only $0.06 cents.

As you can corroborate in the following link: https://www. buybitcoinworldwide.com/price/

It is known that the Bitcoin was created by Satoshi Nakamoto, and we say that this is what is said because that is just a pseudonym, not the real name of who prefers or those who prefer to protect their identity, not only to avoid major problems, but because the identity of its creator has no major relevance, since Bitcoin is like a creature that once created and manages itself, it cannot be stopped. Bitcoin, like all cryptocurrencies that exist today, was born with a series of advantages that differentiate it from the rest of the currencies we know today, even those of greater renown such as the Dollar and the Euro.

At that time, many people invested, but in reality, we could say that they are few in comparison with those who today regret not having done it at that time. By that time it was not easy to bet on a currency that was not controlled by any bank or any state, because that is what Cryptocurrencies are, virtual currencies over which no government or banking entity has any kind of control and whose value increases or decreases according to its fluctuation in the market, that is, according to the said golden law of the economy and the free market, that which says that things acquire greater value when their demand raises the supply, and that will decrease when the supply exceeds the demand. As simple as that.

Now, why use Bitcoin or any of the other Cryptocurrencies that exist in the market, when there are already several electronic means of payment such as PayPal, Neteller, Stripe, among many others? Because Cryptocurrencies do not need intermediaries. In order to pay someone through PayPal you need to enter the platform of that currency and make the transaction, for which you will be charged a commission in addition to losing some time complying with all its rules and requirements that sometimes become very tedious.

With Bitcoin, as with any other cryptocurrency, you are spared this annoying step thanks to the peer-to-peer modality, or in other words, person to person. The only ones who will know about the transaction will be you and the other person, no one else. There is no need to involve any other person or intermediary.

We will give you a very punctual example with things that are very fashionable in the current world of electronic transactions to give you an idea of how Cryptocurrencies work:

IMAGINE YOU HAVE A BUSINESS IDEA, you want to sell sporting goods, but you want them to be sold worldwide, you want them to go far. Well, the first thing you will do is to hire people to create a website, fill it with interesting content and publish your sporting goods to be sold worldwide, so anyone in any country, could enter your online store (which will be your website) and they can pay you for any item that interests them, of those that you will sell there.

Well, those employees that you will need in the beginning, you will only need them in the first moment, to start, then your business by itself will be able to work in the wonderful world of the internet. Those employees that you are going to hire, are not people that you need to see in person, they can be freelancers that you hire through classified job sites, so you can end up hiring a copywriter, a translator, a web designer and a graphic designer. With those four professionals you will be able to create your entire web business and start selling your articles.

Both the articles you will sell and the fees of those freelance workers can be paid with Cryptocurrencies. You pay them with that currency, and in turn you will also receive that currency for each customer who buys your sporting goods.

That's how the world is starting to work, and that's where the new era of global economic markets is heading, where banks and payment platforms will no longer be needed. You pay your workers directly, and your customers pay you in the same way. Isn't that wonderful? This way we save a fortune in almost unnecessary commissions thanks to the birth of Cryptocurrencies.

By all these, you may also be wondering if Bitcoin and Cryptocurrencies are really a legal thing. Well, it turns out that even the Central Bank itself asked the same question, and the truth is that they have no way of saying that it is not. There are many countries where it is still not legal to use this type of currencies, but not because some kind of fraud has occurred, but because it is a currency that no government or any agency will be able to control, they prefer not to involve it in their market, which makes us suspect that what really worries them is that they will not have power over it, but as you can see, Cryptocurrencies have come to stay and that nothing and no one will be able to stop it when it has been established in the whole world.

Now, as we were telling you a few lines ago, the early adopters (as they call the first people who dare to invest in a new product) of Cryptocurrencies today are millionaires thanks to Bitcoin. We are talking about people who invested very little money for a few or even thousands of Bitcoin back in 2009 and today have a fortune thanks to it.

Let's go first with the example of the young Norwegian university student, Kristoffer Koch, he invested approximately a little less than $30 in Bitcoin to use as a sample for his thesis defense.

What was his thesis about? Well, what we are telling you about in this book, Cryptocurrencies as a free and independent means of payment that does not need intermediaries. What happened? That Koch defended his thesis, graduated, and forgot about his Bitcoins. Back in 2014, when he realized that the famous Bitcoin was making headlines all the time, he went, retrieved his key and password, and saw that his Bitcoins were worth a fortune. He had 5,600 BTC, sold 80% and bought a luxury apartment. Today a single Bitcoin can be worth up to $19,000, while Koch tries not to think about that, because with what he bought an apartment in 2014, he could buy a whole building today. But that's the point, everyone is free to do with their money as they see fit. That is the beauty of cryptocurrencies, the financial freedom of those who own them.

Another very famous case in the media is that of teenager Erik Finman, he was 12 years old when his grandmother gave him $1,000 dollars as a birthday present. Do you know what he did with that money? He invested it in Bitcoin. As the years went by, the currency acquired the value we already mentioned and today, without being of age yet, Erik is a multimillionaire. However, just as it goes up, the value of Bitcoin can also go down, and that is something he is aware of, so he has been thinking of selling a little at a time if the market depreciates too much.

As you can see, it's not a fairy tale affair. The world of cryptocurrencies, like any other business, has its risks. Therefore, it is very important to stay informed and that is the goal we want to accomplish with this book, to offer you all the information possible so that you can learn about this new era of Cryptocurrencies that is here to stay and so you can make the most of it.

The Cryptocurrency market has evolved so much that those cases we mentioned are just a few isolated ones, today there are tycoons who live by moving their money in different Cryptocurrencies, including Ethereum, and others that we will mention later, but the fact is that so far, although many have acquired a very high value, few have gone as far as the Bitcoin. The truth is that all those people who invested in Bitcoin when it started are today multimillionaires, if they were not fools and sold them early when they were still not worth anything.

IF YOU WANT to know a case of someone who was very smart, we'll tell you about 50 cents, the famous rapper you probably know beforehand. It turns out that 50 cents released an album in 2014 where he allowed his fans to pay in Bitcoin when they bought it.

What happened? That back then Bitcoin was worth about $600 and today it's worth between 6 and 7 figures.

As you can see, there is no way for you to be an early adopter anymore because Bitcoin has skyrocketed globally, it is no longer something new without value, quite the contrary, it has become an almost exquisite currency. However, that doesn't mean you can't acquire it. It's all a matter of knowing how to make the right moves. There are many ways to get Bitcoins right now, but not everyone knows about them. We will be talking about them in other chapters later, for now the important thing is that you know that they exist, that it is not a lie, that it is a real world despite being virtual currencies and that just as other people have become rich, it can happen to you too, it is just a matter of, as we said at the beginning of this chapter, being as informed as possible and being creative when making your financial moves, that is, knowing when and how to invest your money in Cryptocurrencies that will later increase in value. That is where the secret lies.

There are many reasons to enter this world, and the first one we already showed you, Bitcoin and Cryptocurrencies are real, they exist, they are not a hoax and they are here to stay, however, we will give you some other reasons in case you are still not completely convinced, although we believe that once you have read the anecdotes of ordinary people who invested in Bitcoin and are now multi-millionaires, you will probably be very interested in the matter, sure you will be.

However, in addition to the fact that it is economically worthwhile, we want to tell you that Cryptocurrencies have computer systems that prevent them from being counterfeited or stolen, therefore, we are talking about a reliable economic system.

Another very interesting detail about the Bitcoin is that it is a currency that not only can be bought but also can be mined. This topic of Bitcoin mining is a bit complex but not complicated, so we do not want to saturate you with information and we prefer to prepare this information in a more condensed way so that you can understand it very easily in a chapter that is later in this book.

Anonymity is perhaps another reason why you might be interested in Bitcoin. What is that all about? Well, it turns out that in order to use this cryptocurrency you just need to have a computer, download the Bitcoin software and create your account. That account doesn't need to have any personal information about you, it's just a kind of locker to send and receive Bitcoin. You don't need to give your name, you don't need to know the name of other users, you just need to have an account, and the person who will pay you in Bitcoin will do it there. The same will happen if you need to pay something in that currency.

As you can see, the only possible disadvantage is that since it is not something physical, it is not tangible coins or bills that you can take with you to the beach and buy an ice cream on the sand, but if you have your virtual locker and the seller of halados also has it, just by making a transfer from your cell phone or laptop, you can pay him and he can get paid immediately. We insist, it is a virtual currency to charge by transfers and pay in the same way, isn't it wonderful to never have to use cash again and to be able to pay for everything with just one click?

. . .

IF ALL THIS topic seems interesting to you, we invite you to continue reading the rest of the chapters we have written in this book for you, because we have done it for all the people who are interested in learning about Cryptocurrencies despite knowing nothing or very little about them.

2

UNDERSTANDING BLOCKCHAIN AND BITCOIN TRANSACTIONS

As we mentioned in the previous chapter, Bitcoin electronic transactions, as in the rest of the cryptocurrencies, take place from person to person, without intermediaries, which in the world of cryptocurrencies is known as *"peer to peer"*.

Now, specifically for Bitcoin, its creator, Satoshi Nakamoto, has called Blockchain that interesting and complex virtual construction that is woven as people pass Bitcoins from one account to another.

The blockchain is nothing more than what is being built on the network with each Bitcoin payment or collection. At first the term was used only for this cryptocurrency, but the system has been so successful that the rest of the cryptocurrencies have begun to use it and nowadays it is said that all of them use the blockchain system.

The blockchain is something like a ledger, it is the record that exists in the network of each transaction. If you pay someone with Bitcoin or some other cryptocurrency like Ethereum, for example, that at once will be recorded on the network, the same thing will happen when that person uses those Bitcoin to pay someone else, and so on.

The interesting thing about blockchains is that they are anony-mous, you don't need to say what you used those crypto assets for, let alone give your real data. Blockchains are kind of like a ledger where you can write down everything but you can't erase anything. It is a very ingenious way to ensure that there is no cheating or forgery, If you spent your Bitcoins, there will be no way to reverse that, and if you want to get them back you will have no choice but to earn them by working or investing in them, buying more Bitcoins.

Even though those transactions reflected as blockchains are anonymous, that does not mean they are private. Everyone can have access to them, including obviously the participants of the transactions, who automatically get a certified copy to keep their personal records and be able to keep track of their assets.

That's right, although this seems out of control, it is not. Just because banks and governments can't intervene in Bitcoin transactions, doesn't mean we're talking about a crazy, messy thing. Did it occur to you that people could pay $19,000 for something crazy and meaningless? Well, if you thought, you are very wrong.

Why are blockchains necessary? Well, it's pretty obvious, if there is no control whatsoever, there is a need for a reliable registry that allows people to dare to invest in this currency, or pay/collect in it, whatever you want to call it.

People making transactions with Bitcoin are not rosy characters from a fairy tale that everyone trusts everyone just because, in fact people have been known to use this means of payment for illegal things, but that does not mean there have been scams, but simply that there is no way to track where the money comes from and where it goes to, which makes it all a very interesting topic for many markets, including illegal markets.

Blockchains make it so that a Bitcoin that has already been spent cannot be reused by the same user. That is what blockchains are for, as we already said, to keep a record.

Now that we have talked about what is now a reality, it is good to remember that in 2008, a decade ago, when the creator of Bitcoin announced that he was formalizing all this that we know today as blockchain, nobody believed in it, nobody bet on it, they thought it was some kind of delirium, some kind of madness, and some even thought it would be a failure and even said that it would all be a fraud, a scam.

Today, a decade later, we can see that it is all real. We in this book ask you:

Don't you think it's time to ask yourself where all this is pointing to in the future?

Well, it turns out that several computer scientists have studied blockchains and have recognized that it is a magnificent system for recording transactions, and most agree that it is a matter of time before the registry invented by the creator of Bitcoin becomes a system that adapts to all types of markets so that transactions are no longer mediated by banks, companies, businesses and other intermediary organizations.

In other words, it seems that not only cryptocurrencies, including Bitcoin, are here to stay, but also that their systems, their ways of working are so great that the other markets, the traditional ones, those that have already been established for hundreds of years, will end up adopting systems such as blockchains.

WHY? You might ask, and we would tell you that the answer is obvious and we are surprised that you are asking that question. Isn't it great that there is a record of transactions where no more information has to be entered than the transaction data itself, where no one is cheated, where everything is very clear, and where no one can cheat or erase what has already been done?

Imagine that this is how all transactions would be nowadays, imagine that this is how everything would be paid for, imagine not having to enter your passport data, not having to stand in a long queue at a bank to open an account and then having to ask the bank for permission every time you want to use your money and that it is very problematic at times to obtain data on what you have paid or spent.

That is the blockchain, the solution to all these problems, and we in this book are betting that this is where the market will be heading in the coming years.

On the other hand, to continue telling you about the advantages of blockchain, we can tell you about the financial part, the part where you save more thanks to this new system that was invented with Bitcoin and that seems to be used in all transactions in the future.

WHAT IS the idea of saving more by making blockchain transfers?

WELL, by making person-to-person transfers without any bank in between, without any intermediary, we are automatically eliminating a collector in the economic chain, i.e. we are dispensing with an employee who gets paid as the owner.

We will not name names. But there are banks, exchange houses and other companies that provide support for electronic transactions, which charge commissions ranging from 7% to 20% of the amount transacted. In other words, you can pay $100 to someone, and if that someone gets even $80, that's quite a lot. Does that sound fair to you? Maybe the owner of the company would say yes because it is what they need to charge to maintain the platform, but the truth is that it is a business. We don't think it's wrong, but we don't think that's better than blockchain either.

With blockchain transactions you forget about having to pay those expensive fees and you get what they sent you, as well as that person you are paying gets what you sent them.

On the other hand, another advantage of blockchain is that every-thing is decentralized, i.e. there is no single platform or source through which to access the information that makes Bitcoin transfers possible. If Bitcoin were tied to a centralized network, it would be enough for that network to have a failure for us to stop being able to transfer in that cryptocurrency.

For blockchain transfers to be affected, the Internet service would have to be down worldwide, something that has not happened so far, not even when there was talk of the dark phenomenon of Y2K, which we all know ended up being more media terrorism than anything else.

Now, this whole blockchain issue gives way to what Bitcoin mining is all about. It turns out that all the electronic framework that is generated in the blockchain with each new transaction, in turn generates new codes, each one is unique and unrepeatable, that is what makes transactions fair and secure, hence the importance of this blockchain system that does not give rise to scams.

BITCOIN MINERS ARE computers that have been predisposed to try to solve the algorithms that are generated in the complex and tangled world of blockchain. That world is complex if you try to analyze it as a normal person, trying to understand how everything is organized in that electronic universe. However, for a person who only adds a block, that is, who only makes the transactions he/she wants and nothing else, there is nothing complicated about it.

Bitcoin miners seek to solve these puzzles because the creators of Bitcoin have decided to reward those who succeed. This is done because in various ways they can contribute to the development of this type of networks and because they make contributions that, from a computer science point of view, are extremely valuable.

However, it is not at all easy to achieve this. In a future chapter, later in this book, we will give you more details. For now, the important thing is for you to know that blockchains are the system by which all Bitcoin transactions are recorded, in a medium that is public and anonymous at the same time, where there is practically no risk of cheating or scams and where everything is very clear, without confusion for ordinary users like you, who will soon open your Bitcoin locker and start making transactions in this famous cryptocurrency that is so much talked about nowadays.

3

BITCOIN FOR BEGINNERS, WHERE DO I START?

F irst of all, I would like to tell you that nowadays there are many websites where you can check the prices of all your cryptocurrencies in real time, one of the most recommended is CoinMarketCap which you can visit at the following link:

HTTPS://COINMARKETCAP.COM/

NOW THAT YOU know all the basic things about Bitcoin, that is, what it is, how it started, what is its history, and all those interesting details about the most famous cryptocurrency nowadays, it is time for you to start learning about how to get started in it, how to get your own Bitcoin locker or wallet and start saving in what is so far the most secure and reliable cryptocurrency in the crypto asset market for almost a decade now. As we mentioned in the previous chapter, it all started when Satoshi Nakamoto published the "Bitcoin White Paper" and then launched the website www.bitcoin.org to publicize the project, which is still up and running today and you can visit it. If you are interested in reading the Bitcoin white paper in English you can do it in the following link:

SEE THE BITCOIN WHITEPAPER HERE:
https://bitcoin.org/en/bitcoin-paper

BACK TO OUR TOPIC, the first step is to download the Bitcoin application so you can make use of Bitcoin per-sé. Remember that you can do it either on your computer or on your cell phone. We particularly recommend that you do it on your cell phone because you can make transactions from wherever you want, while if you do it only on your computer, you can only do it from home or office. However, the more daring ones usually install it on both, and that is also an option.

What you are going to download and install on your computers is what is known as the client application, the one that will allow you to move forward in the Bitcoin world. It is good that you know that it works with almost any operating system, among which are Windows, Mac, Linux, among others, so as you can see, it works for the established systems in the market and also for those who wish to work with free or open-source software and you can find it here:

HTTPS://BITCOIN.ORG/EN/CHOOSE-YOUR-WALLET

YOU JUST HAVE to choose the Bitcoin Core version (the official version) and download it by selecting your operating system. For example, this is the version for Windows:

HTTPS://BITCOIN.ORG/EN/CHOOSE-YOUR-WALLET?STEP=1&PLATFORM=
WINDOWS

. . .

LIKE ALMOST ANYTHING ELSE, once the application is installed on your device, it is time to create your user, or what in Bitcoin is called wallet. That will be a space where you will be able to monitor and manipulate the money you have in Bitcoin. It is similar to having a money account in a bank, but you will not have to wait days or even weeks to open an account or have to wait in an endless queue or have to provide all that cumbersome paperwork.

With Bitcoin you can create your own wallet and start managing Bitcoins on your own, directly with the other users you'll be transacting with. Fortunately, Bitcoin is so great that it offers several options for you to choose the one that best suits your tastes and needs.

You can install some of the basic wallets, those that are very easy to download, such as: Bitcoin QT, Armory and Multibit. Any of the three wallets we have just mentioned are programs to be installed on computers.

If on the other hand you prefer to install any of the wallets that are to work online, that is, to make your transactions directly from the Internet, there are also options that are to please those tastes, as perfectly can be: Blockchain, Coinbase, coinjar and coinpunk.

The only detail why we could recommend you a fixed installation one instead of one to work online, is that the first ones are usually more secure, but we know that online wallets are usually preferred by users because they are easier and simpler to use, so they end up being more friendly.

Well, once you have decided which modality to use, it is time to take action and carry out the most important step, that of finally putting your wallet to work.

I PERSONALLY USE the www.bitcoin.com application on my cell phone which you can download from the Apple Store if you have an iPhone or from the Play Store if you have an Android phone. In the following link you will find the wallets offered by Bitcoin.com:

.   .   .

HTTPS://WALLET.BITCOIN.COM/

DO NOT CONFUSE www.bitcoin.org with www.bitcoin.com the first website is the one created in 2009 by Satoshi Nakamoto and the second by the founder Roger Ver, both are reliable options, although Bitcoin.com offers portability, the Bitcoin.org version is more complex to configure because you need more computer knowledge.

BELOW WE DESCRIBE step by step how to create your wallet and set it up immediately so you can receive and store your Bitcoins in an easy, simple, convenient and, above all, very secure way:

THE MOST USUAL WAY, or the one that many recommend, is to create a Cold Wallet, or what in English would be a cold wallet. This is one of the most used methods by most users because it is very simple and of all those that exist, it seems to be the safest.

To create a Cold Wallet, the steps are as follows:

FIRST YOU MUST CREATE your private key, remember that although there are no major requirements to create Bitcoin accounts, it is important that your account is yours, private, and therefore you must create a security key that is very easy to remember but that only you can recognize. A password that you can't forget but at the same time that no one else can guess. Nobody wants to go through life believing that they have their Bitcoins well secured and then one morning find out that someone else knew the key, had access, and took them.

The way to generate the key is to go to the Bitcoin address page, i.e. bitaddress.org, and there you will click on the option to enable randomization. This step is mandatory but at the same time it is very simple, you just have to place the cursor over that option and wait for it to reach the required total, that is, to reach the 100% that is required for it. You will notice it through a small bar that will be loaded on your screen and it will announce you when it has reached the exact number of 100%.

THE COLD WALLET, once you generate the randomness in the previous step, will give you two keys, one private and one public. Just by seeing that you can save your data, reserve that key somewhere secret, and with that you are good to go. However, we know that there are people who need or prefer to have something physical, something they can see, that certifies the step they have taken. For those people there is the Paper Wallet, which is a kind of sheet that certifies the step taken and that you can get just by clicking on the top menu option once the Cold Wallet is created.

WASN'T IT QUITE SIMPLE? Too easy, we think. As we told you before, creating a Bitcoin wallet is something very easy and simple and at the same time a super secure way to manage your Bitcoins, unless you give away your password, that is, that private, secret key that Bitcoin gives you once you create your wallet.

Whenever you make transactions, you can check if they have been made on the www.Blockchain.com/explorer website, just enter the transaction number.

HOW CAN YOU KEEP YOUR ACCOUNT SECURE?

There is one thing you can share with anyone you want and that is your Bitcoin wallet address, you can put it on your private profile, on your social networks, on your TL on Twitter or on your Facebook wall. The address of your wallet is public and you can share it with anyone you want, you will still have to do it when making any kind of transaction with any other user.

What you should never do if you do not want to be unwary, is to share your secret password. The name itself says it, it is secret, private, only yours. You should not share it with anyone. We think this is pretty obvious but it is worth emphasizing. Anyone who has your secret key (also known as SEED, has your Bitcoins).

Well, once you have everything set up, it's time to start holding Bitcoin, and you may be wondering how to start holding that famous cryptocurrency in your wallet. Well, the first thing you can do is go to the direct method of buying Bitcoin from anyone, anyone who is selling Bitcoin.

Remember that thanks to peer to peer and blockchain, you can buy and sell Bitcoin directly without the slightest middleman and without having to pay a penny in commissions.

For example, you can buy Bitcoins on this reliable website without any problem:

Go to Coinbase and buy Bitcoins Here:

The detail is that by the time this book is being published, the Bitcoin is in one of its best moments. It is no longer like it was in 2009 when Bitcoin was just getting started. Now, right now, Bitcoin is at a pretty high value, so there won't be much you can buy if you don't have a large amount of money. However, we will still explain how to do it in case you are interested, want and can buy Bitcoin, which is perhaps the fastest and most direct way to have this cryptocurrency in your wallet.

It is important for you to know that once you have downloaded the application to create your wallet, you must download an additional one that you must synchronize with your account. This new application is the one that will allow you to make transactions, that is, we are talking about a new application just to be able to add blocks. Remember that as we explained in previous chapters, transactions between Bitcoin users are recorded in a kind of gigantic public ledger called blockchain, and each new transaction is a new encrypted block, unique and unrepeatable that is added to the blockchain.

For you to be able to add a new block to the chain, that is, so that you can make a new transaction, what you must do is download the app for it and follow the instructions that will appear on the screen. Once you have followed all the steps, you just have to add both your public key and your private key, and that's it, you can buy and sell Bitcoin from your cell phone, your laptop or any computer where you want.

As we know that at this moment the Bitcoin has a high value, we recommend you to buy a minimum amount, something fractional. One of the advantages is that you do not need to buy or pay for a full Bitcoin, you can buy a minimum fraction in decimals, and as you are starting, our suggestion is that this fraction is really minimal, at least until you become familiar with this and you feel really comfortable with the subject of buying and selling Bitcoins.

Just as you can buy Bitcoins, you can also sell them. This is one of the most common ways people keep doing Bitcoin transactions. With the Cold Wallet you can handle large amounts of Bitcoin, we recommend you to start with small amounts for the reasons we already explained, but you don't have to limit yourself once you get the hang of it and know how to operate and make transactions, if you decide you want to buy more and more.

If you want to store your Bitcoins in something other than a wallet, you have the option of Exchange sites, but we don't particularly recommend it. Exchange sites are an excellent option when it comes to selling your Bitcoins if you don't want to deal with or find a buyer yourself. The problem with these sites is that they operate just like a bank, they do the work for you, they look for the buyer, but at the same time they will obviously charge you a commission for it and you will have lost the fun of blockchain because you will be using an intermediary. It is not bad to start with, but we want to tell you that nowadays there are many forums where Bitcoin buyers and sellers meet on the internet, so it may not be too difficult to find a buyer or seller, whatever the case of what you are looking for.

IF YOU DO NOT WANT to access these forums for fear of fraud, we remind you that blockchains are extremely secure, and as long as you do not reveal your private key, it is almost impossible for you to be a victim of some kind of theft. That is, no one is exempt from scams almost anywhere, but you would have to be really too careless for something like that to happen to you through the blockchain, because it would not be about being a victim of a fraud or some kind of software or program that would steal your money, but it would be that you would sin of overconfidence, and with that there is no security system that is worth. In other words, it would be up to you if you let yourself be swindled in this way.

On the other hand, as we said at the beginning of this chapter, there are also hot wallets, which are those that are already online, i.e., those for which you do not need to download anything else to be able to use them. We do not recommend this type of wallets because, being hot wallets that are already connected, they are spaces where you will have to provide your data, i.e. your passwords, all the time, and we know the disadvantages of that. That is to say, we prefer to recommend cold wallets because they are much more secure.

IN OTHER WORDS, both wallets can be secure, but when it comes to making a comparison to choose one or the other, the cold wallet ends up winning. Now, it remains to tell you about the wallets or purses that are in the cloud.

Just like the hot wallets or wallets, you do not need to download anything and you can use it in a very easy and simple way, but we still recommend the wallets that are downloaded because of the privacy they offer.

Finally on the subject of wallets we want to talk about what is perhaps the most innovative: the wallets for smartphones that have an Exchange built in. Yes, as you have read, you download the app on your cell phone and immediately you have how to trade, that is, how to buy and sell your Bitcoins. All from your cell phone. We have already told you that we do not recommend this option because of the issue of commissions, that is, to avoid the figure of the intermediary, but we must admit that it is too comfortable that option that from your cell phone, from the same application, you can do everything immediately. So that comfort and ease obviously has to have a price, and if you are willing to pay it, who are we to prevent it?

As we have already shown you the different options that exist, we will show you some specific examples of the different wallets that you can use. That is to say, we already told you the types of wallets that exist, now we will give you specific examples of the different brands that exist in the market, the different portals that you can access depending on your case:

For hot or online wallets:

Blockchain is quite an interesting example because besides being hot, that is, being online immediately, it also offers a mobile version, so if you want to do everything from your Smartphone, this is an interesting option.

Coinbase is perhaps the most famous and you can see it in the following link:

. . .

BUY BITCOINS AT COINBASE HERE:

As you know we have already mentioned it a few paragraphs ago, and it is undoubtedly the one that has the most users because it is the most secure and reliable currently. This hot wallet has the particularity that it is open to everyone as a wallet, that is, as a space to store your Bitcoins. However, if you want to sell Bitcoins from this App, you can do it, but it is only valid for the United States and Europe, for now, although it is rumored that the company that launched it has strong intentions to expand this option so that just as the whole world can use it as a wallet to store virtual money, i.e. Bitcoins, they can also do it when trading Bitcoin, i.e. to sell them.

ELEKTRUM IS the fastest one on the market, because we are not going to lie to you, downloading wallets on your laptop or desktop computer is usually a bit tedious because most of them require you to download a complete blockchain. In this option, you don't need to have to download something so heavy, and thus it becomes the best option if you don't have much storage space, or if you simply don't have the patience to wait for such a heavy download.

CarbonWallet is not very well known, but it has the interesting feature of offering access to the desktop once you install it on your PC without the need to be connected to the internet. We recommend it for those who do not always have internet access and want to work from the computer.

. . .

STRONGCOIN IS PERHAPS the most popular when it comes to hybrid wallets. A hybrid wallet is one that allows you to connect online or work through its own application and this specific application is a perfect example of how you can have the best of both worlds.

For those who prefer to install something of their own on their desktop or laptop, there are also interesting options, as we described in this article. It's time to recommend you the ones that exist in the market, giving you a little critical but objective view so that we can somehow offer you lights when choosing one or the other.

BITCOIN-QT IS PERHAPS the best or most famous of the options for computers, but as we explained to you in the previous point, it has the disadvantage that you compulsorily need to download a complete blockchain. However, the sacrifice or hassle is worth it because once you download all that you will have access to direct databases that Bitcoin, that is, if you love Bitcoin, if you want to have the best of Bitcoin, this is the best option because in addition to all that gives you direct access to make direct peer to peer transactions, that is, through the blockchain system.

ARMORY IS a wallet for which you first need to install the previous one, i.e. Bitcoin-qt. If with that one you have the best of Bitcoin, with this one you take it to the highest level, because this option is more for meticulous users who want to increase their security level. It's not that anything bad has happened with the original basic function, but simply that there are users who are a bit more demanding, and Bitcoin has decided to launch this for them, the most exquisite when it comes to security.

Hive is one of the newest options, it is exclusive to Mac and connects you directly to the app store to deal with Bitcoin merchants.

So, if you are a Mac user and want to have the newest and most practical feature they have released for Bitcoin, this is for you, although we do not know how it will develop, because at the time of writing this book, this function was still in the process of evolution, or testing period, or whatever you want to call the Beta stage.

DARK WALLET IS a version that is also in the testing period, and its main feature is that it offers extreme privacy. That is, not only does it give you the normal anonymity that blockchains already offer, but it even makes it impossible to trace the user's address. Perfect, for now, for all those who are pretty picky about wanting to stay hidden from all sorts of trackers. Some users have reported interest in it to protect their identity in the case that they are users who move very large amounts of Bitcoin and do not want to risk their physical security and not only that of their Bitcoin account.

MULTIBIT IS ideal for those who do not want to download a whole blockchain, because with this option you only download the header and so you can make your transactions, but obviously you will not have much access to other things, but it is fine for those who want to go straight to the point, plus it works with all operating systems, which has made it quite popular in recent years.

FINALLY, we bring you the recommendations when it comes to smartphones:

BITCOINWALLET IS SO FAR the most famous and the most successful of the options out there for Android and it's online. So, if you want something more downloadable and less online, this is not necessarily the best option for you, although as you can see, it is the most downloaded for smartphones. You download it from here:

. . .

HTTPS://WALLET.BITCOIN.COM/

COPAY IS the option that allows you to use cellular numbers as a public Bitcoin address. If you are a person who likes to synchronize with google and have everything registered from the contacts database of your cell phone, this option is ideal and perfect for you.

MICELLIUM IS from the same creators of Bitcoin wallet but it is more like a kind of complement. It is still in a testing period in some of its functions, although there are users who claim that they do not need to test anything and that it is the best thing that has come on the market.

Well, since we have shown you our recommendations in the shortest possible way to help you make decisions when opening a Bitcoin wallet, it is good that you know the dark side, the world of scams that have existed in Bitcoin.

Contrary to what you may think, it is not that we have lied to you, because Bitcoin with its blockchain system really offers a very safe way to make transactions where virtually all transactions are safe and reliable from the electronic point of view, also offering an interesting anonymity that protects your identity to avoid other types of crimes and offenses.

It turns out that the biggest scams that have happened in Bitcoin, have really been due to a matter of ignorance on the part of users, and below we will show you examples of the most notorious cases worldwide:

Precisely because of the security and anonymity provided by Bitcoin transaction systems, in Australia some fraudsters posing as tax collection companies have managed to steal thousands of dollars so far. How do they do it? Well, they trick people into believing they have a debt to pay, and offer them the facility to do so through

Bitcoin. People get scammed, end up sending Bitcoin to accounts that can hardly be traced, and then lose their money with impunity because there is no way to find the whereabouts of that money.

Another cryptocurrency that operates in a very similar way Bitcoin, as is Ethereum, has registered almost 700 scams to date, and all in the same way they have scammed people with Bitcoin.

These scams occur precisely thanks to the ease of paying in cryptocurrency. They trick you, make you believe that you must make a very cumbersome mandatory payment and then offer you an alternative how with even discounts for speed. If you are convinced that you must pay something expensive in a very cumbersome way, it would not be unusual for you to accept the first offer in which they lower the costs of that debt and also provide you with the means to do so.

Where does the scam really occur?

In believing that you are serious about making those payments. As you can see, Bitcoin and cryptocurrencies in general lend themselves to this kind of thing, but as we have argued throughout this chapter in this book, if you are unwary or ignorant, there is not much we can do for you, which is why we created this book with the best of intentions to keep you as informed as possible and thus not only avoid these problems but you can get the most out of Bitcoin, whatever way you decide to operate.

4

WHERE CAN I BUY BITCOIN?

I n the previous chapter we emphasized that we did not recommend Exchange sites to open a wallet, insisting that the most advisable when opening an account to trade Bitcoin, was to download an application on your computer, tablet, laptop or even cell phone, or else work from online spaces that also offer these services.

However, that was with regard to creating your purse or wallet, that is, to create that space to be able to access the Bitcoin. When it comes to the space where to look for Bitcoin sellers, the matter may be different, especially if you are a novice and do not know anyone in the Bitcoin trading environment, because we know that this of buying and selling Bitcoin is a huge market with which you may not feel familiar yet, especially if you are a beginner, and it is not bad, at first, go to the platforms that make things easier, despite having to deal with commissions of intermediaries.

Below we detail the sites where you can buy Bitcoin, as well as their respective commission rates so you can be aware of how much you have to pay in addition to the purchase of each Bitcoin, so that this does not take you by surprise and then do not think you're being scammed. If you go to these places and sell Bitcoin, do not come later to say that we did not warn you that you had to pay an additional commission.

COINBASE

IT IS THE MOST FAMOUS, no one can deny it. It is a platform that allows you to use credit or debit cards to exchange your euros or dollars for Bitcoins at a rate imposed by them and with a commission that they also impose.

YOU CAN BUY **Bitcoin and other Cryptocurrencies here:**

This platform to buy Bitcoins offers many facilities as mentioned above, plus it has support for more than 30 countries around the world, and to date has managed to have been traded on its website more than $ 20,000,000,000,000 dollars that have ended up invested in Bitcoin. Reasons enough to consider it a fairly reliable platform, in addition to the fact that to date no one has reported a scam by this company selling Bitcoin.

This platform has many payment methods, has been operating since 2012 in the United States and is gaining more and more followers because it no longer sells only Bitcoin but has also added other cryptocurrencies that are not as popular as Bitcoin but still represent an alternative for many people worldwide, such as Ethereum, among other cryptocurrencies.

As if all these benefits were not enough, this platform offers a free wallet service, although as you know, we will always recommend you to use your own personal wallet. However, the idea of having every-thing within the same page is still attractive, and if you think about it, it makes a lot of sense to want to be able to do everything by opening a single tab in the browser.

If you like this platform, we must also tell you that it offers a free virtual wallet for cell phones, you just have to download it at no cost, after all, it is in their interest to get you hooked, so they offer you that facility.

But not everything is so perfect, because as we have already explained, this type of sites charge commission, and this platform is no exception. In addition to charging something, they have the highest rate, that is to say, they are the one that takes the most money from you for each transaction. Their policies explain that they charge 1% of each transaction you make, but the truth is that they have a series of internal rules that even lead to the fact that you actually have to pay almost 4% at the end of the story.

CEX.IO

IT IS another quite old platform, we could even say that it has more time in the Bitcoin market than the previous platform, despite the fact that she is today more famous. However, this platform that we present you at the moment has also a very good portfolio of customers, every time there are millions and millions of users regis-tered on it and also has an excellent reputation, allowing you to buy Bitcoins on it through Euros and Dollars. You can visit it and buy Cryptocurrencies in the following link:

. . .

Visit **CEX.IO and see the prices here:**

This platform allows you to use your own cold wallet, it works for all countries in the world, except Vietnam. It is a platform with a great reputation where no one has registered any kind of scam, it is preferred by many because it is the easiest to use, since to buy Bitcoins on it, basically you just need to make several clicks, and its commissions are lower than those of the competition, being always quite varied according to different cases, but it never reaches 3%, even very rarely reaches half of that.

LocalBitcoins

It was created in 2012, almost 23 years after Bitcoin emerged. This is an interesting platform although it is not highly recommended for beginners, it is more for people who without really needing to be all experts, at least master the basics of the Cryptocurrency market, especially Bitcoin. You can see the website here:

Visit **LocalBitcoins and see the prices here:**
       https://localbitcoins.com/es/?ch=x5bv

.   .   .

BASICALLY, this is the best platform to make use of one of the maximum advantages of Bitcoin, such as Peer to Peer transactions, or P2P as they are also called. The creator of this platform opened it with the intention of not using intermediaries and not paying commissions, so once you decide to buy Bitcoins on it, you should not pay anything extra, but as we said just a few lines ago, if you are a beginner, it can be a little confusing, plus you have to deal with the typical of an open market where not everyone has the same rates and not all sellers are equally professional.

However, like the rest of the platforms, it operates in almost all countries and allows the use of traditional payment currencies such as the dollar and the Euro.

Coinmama

IT WAS FOUNDED in 2013 and is since then one of the most used platforms, although it does not beat the ones we have mentioned above, for various reasons, however, that is not a reason to distrust it, it is just that it has some small limitations that the others do not, plus it does not have so much fame and popularity, and we know that this is not necessarily an indicator of low quality, it is just a matter of marketing and propaganda in which it cannot compete with others much larger in that sense. Visit it at the following link:

VISIT COINMAMA and see prices here:
http://go.coinmama.com/visit/?bta=54429&nci=5360

THIS PLATFORM OFFERS MORE security than the rest because you are not really buying Bitcoin from any user. In fact, this platform does not allow selling or buying Bitcoin between users, but the platform itself, that is, the company itself is who sells them to you and who buys them from you. In short, this company has created a space to centralize the purchase and sale of Bitcoin, and if you do not have problems with that, we present it as a very viable alternative when buying Bitcoin with credit or debit card or even from Western Union for those who have or wish to pay their Bitcoins from that means of payment.

The low popularity of this platform compared to the others is based in part on the fact that they can charge you a very low commission, but if you buy Bitcoin or Ethereum with a credit card, they can take up to 6% of the amount you sell or buy in transactions, which in turn are limited to a maximum of $5,000 per day and $20,000 per month, in terms of the value of Bitcoin.

For its part, one of the advantages is that it accepts almost any type of credit card, which makes it attractive for some countries that usually present difficulties with their platforms in that type of cards, as well as it is also proven that it is the platform where you can buy Bitcoins through credit cards in the fastest way. Some would say that it would be obvious, given the high commissions, but as we have told you before, we believe that the benefits and conveniences have a price and you decide whether to pay it or go for another alternative.

CHANGELLY

IT IS PERHAPS one of the most modern platforms when it comes to buying Bitcoin. It has been in existence for only a couple of years and operates in almost any country in the world, with exceptions in countries where the Internet platform is almost nonexistent.

This platform was initially created to buy Cryptocurrencies through the Cryptocurrencies themselves, that is, to exchange Bitcoins for Ethereum, for example. However, it also offers the alternative of buying Bitcoin through traditional currencies such as dollars and Euros, in addition to accepting electronic payment methods such as PayPal, Neteller, among others. It has a low commission compared to other platforms, which only reach 0.5%. The time it takes for a transaction is very varied and can be quite reasonable, but it does not reach the speed levels of other platforms that have been established for many more years, but it is still very reliable. You can visit here and start shopping:

VISIT CHANGELLY **and see prices here:**
https://changelly.com/?ref_id=oojm7eo13oftnyw2

IT IS HEADQUARTERED IN PRAGUE, but it is fully globalized, to the point that it can operate with any operating system, including Android, among others. It is recommended despite being so new, especially for how well organized it is and how well distributed the information is displayed in its interface. It is set to surpass the other platforms if it continues to improve. Only time will tell.

One last advantage we want to add is that you don't need to register or create an account. You just give the basic data, i.e., you say how much Bitcoin you want to buy, you pay, and that's it, the Bitcoins are yours.

Bitstamp

THIS IS a globetrotting platform that has set up and then moved a couple of times. They started in 2011 in Slovenia, then moved to the UK a couple of years later, and for the last couple of years they have been based in Luxembourg.

This platform is more recommended for experts, and seeks to target buyers and sellers of high amounts, as it offers very low commissions when talking about high figures.

It is shown as one of the safest because it stores most of the clients' money in the well-known cold wallets, however, not many people like it because it does not offer too many alternatives as means of payment.

Anyone can buy cryptocurrencies on this platform, but if you want to do it from a credit card, the company's commission can reach up to 8%, which can have its pros and cons, although as we said before, it is attractive if the amount you are going to acquire is quite high.

BITPANDA

IT IS NOT SO popular worldwide, but we do believe that it is currently one of the most famous in Europe. It accepts as a means of payment almost any electronic currency card, i.e. from PayPal to Neteller, among others.

One of its disadvantages is that the commissions they charge are not made public, but are included in the purchase price when you go to make the transaction. On the other hand, it can almost be said that the only traditional currency they accept is the Euro, which to some extent limits them at an international level.

Other than that, it is one of the most modern and fastest platforms when it comes to buying cryptocurrencies, even though it only works with four of them, including Bitcoin, of course. Transactions for purchases are usually very fast, except when it comes to SEPA which actually takes a whole day. Recommended for beginners, but if you are an expert, you can find better alternatives, more adapted to your tastes and needs.

I personally use for purchases Coinbase, Changelly and in extraordinary cases CEX.io.

FINALLY, we want to add 5 tips before you buy Bitcoin for you to keep in mind before investing in this magnificent cryptocurrency, especially if you are a beginner.

Remember that Bitcoin never sleeps:

Don't stress if for some reason you can't fully monitor a transaction. Cryptocurrencies and almost everything that is generated over the internet, is not like in the real world of 2.0 where there is a day off and a work schedule. Cryptocurrencies are sold around the clock, so don't stress about it, if you need to sleep, you can sleep, and the next day see how your Bitcoin or any other cryptocurrency you are trading is doing.

Get organized:

If you set up an investment plan, your business is much more likely to flow, compared to if you start buying Cryptocurrencies without clear objectives. It is fine to buy Bitcoin in a low amount to start, but that amount, no matter how low it is, must be monitored, taken into account, with profit and loss ranges, with future investment intentions. In short, there are many aspects to consider, but you have the advantage that this investment plan will only be established by yourself, so you can design it according to your interests and your possibilities, thinking about your capabilities and your limitations so that it does not interfere with anything else you think it may affect.

Control everything you invest:

While it is true that Cryptocurrencies have the particularity that they are not controlled by any government or agency as traditional currencies are regulated, you can control how much you spend, that is, how much you invest in each cryptocurrency. We are not the ones to tell you not to buy a certain amount of Bitcoin, for example, but we do recommend that you keep a very well managed control of your investments and that you make them in very organized ways so that you can easily evaluate profits and losses and be able to take timely action when necessary.

. . .

AVOID PANIC:

IF YOU COMPLY with the three previous tips, if you are organized, nothing happens if you lose a certain amount of money, because everything will be under control. There is no need to run to mortgage your house to pay off debts at the first loss. That will only be necessary if you invest absurd amounts and then lose everything because you do not have an adequate control and monitoring of the situation. What you should do is learn from your mistakes, which you will make, because we are human, and especially because you are a beginner. Don't be overwhelmed by that, go ahead, the greatest entrepreneurs also had stumbles and some of them had to start from scratch more than once.

Don't wait too long:

This is the time; this is the opportunity. Although Cryptocurrencies have become famous worldwide, the market has not yet exploited even 20% of what is known to fluctuate, so take advantage of it, invest, but do it taking into account the four previous tips so that this path is one of learning and profit.

5

WHERE TO STORE YOUR BITCOINS THE SAFEST WAY?

I n this chapter we will answer one of the most interesting and, at the same time, one of the most common questions among cryptocurrency users, especially Bitcoin users.

It is not unreasonable that this is one of the most frequently asked questions, after all, this question is for security reasons. If we have taken the step of investing in Bitcoin, the most logical thing is that we want to know where we can store them in the safest way, because no one wants to invest their money and run the risk of losing it all.

These doubts arise in part, because while it is true that the Bitcoin among other cryptocurrencies, is a boom today, with a boom so something that seems that its value does not stop rising, it is also true that there have been scams.

As we have already explained in previous chapters of this book, it is very difficult for Bitcoin to be stolen because of the way it is encrypted. Its creator designed an infallible formula in which, thanks to the blockchain, it is practically impossible to cheat, while it is also very difficult for any computer expert or hacker to apply some kind of trick to steal or alter the transactions that are executed peer to peer.

The problem has come from cryptocurrency buying and selling

platforms where they have really made very foolish and at the same time very serious mistakes, and the consequences have been multi-million-dollar thefts. Once again, we can say, that the insecurity comes neither from the cryptocurrency nor from the techniques in which its creators have generated the possibility of making transactions, but rather from the emerging companies that have joined the market offering services of buying and selling crypto assets, among them the platforms of exchange houses, where such mistakes have the disastrous results that we have already told you about.

Based on these concerns, we have decided to develop a list with all the options that exist in the market for storing Bitcoins, taking into account the most popular ones, because the truth is that there are too many. But we do it with the best intentions to help you make the best decision when choosing a specific wallet or purse to store your Bitcoin.

First of all, we should remind you that there are basically three types of places to store your Bitcoin, but they are all called wallets or purses. To clarify further, wallets or purses do not actually store any money, the money or Bitcoin are actually always in the company's space, in the network. What wallets do is store data that allows you to locate your Bitcoin and organize them, knowing how much you have, how much you have bought and how much you have spent. It may sound a bit complex, especially if you are not very computer literate, but that's what this new era of electronic money is all about where the virtual is actually stored information that you can then, for normal civilized world purposes, convert into real currency or vice versa, because don't forget, Bitcoin and Cryptocurrencies no longer only have a value in dollars and Euros, but you can use them to pay directly as well as to buy for producer or services offered.

The wonderful new world of marketplace 2.0

These virtual wallets are very varied as we have already detailed in some previous chapters, but basically, we remind you that there are 4 main types of wallets or purses, and you choose which one to use.

. . .

ON THE ONE hand we have the online wallets or wallets, which are virtual wallets of the most used today, for a number of conveniences they offer, which seduce almost any Bitcoin user.

On the other hand, there are the offline software wallets, useful for those users who wish to install a wallet that they can use without an internet connection. This is perhaps one of the most recommended for the security and privacy they offer.

We also have the hardware wallets, because it takes the level of security to an even higher point, and is recommended in those cases where high amounts of crypto assets are handled, because being away from the network, that is, being what we also call cold wallets, decreases the levels of electronic theft, which in itself are already quite low in Bitcoin but when it comes to securing our money, it is never enough.

LET'S start with online wallets. We have already told you on several occasions that they are not one of our favorites, but if you are a beginner and you just want to familiarize yourself at a time and then migrate to another when you enter fully into the world of Bitcoins, this can be an interesting option especially because they facilitate everything, or almost everything, making operations simpler, faster and easier.

Coinbase is perhaps the most famous, we have already talked about its benefits in previous chapters, but this time we will take a look at it a little deeper and at the same time more objective, to try to give you the necessary information so you can decide whether to stay with it or choose another option that best suits your tastes and interests.

The only negative detail that we can offer you directly, is that recently it was known that there was a problem with BitcoinCash, which made them lose many followers. However, even with that they are still the most popular today. It has simple and easy to use functions, and that's why everyone uses it. Popularity is not always synonymous with quality, but when it comes to money, it is difficult for people to use a product or service just for fashion.

Blockchain is the second most famous wallet when it comes to online systems. Said by its own users, there is no easier interface to grasp and understand, and many like the advantage that you don't need to register and create an account. You just log in, make your trades, and you're done. There is no major protocol when making use of this famous wallet, so you will surely find it interesting if you want a wallet that does not represent more bureaucracy when moving your Bitcoins, because in this era, time is money.

Apart from these two, there are many other Bitcoin wallets or Cryptocurrency wallets in general that are of this type, online. But the truth is that we will not take them into account for being unpopular, being in trial period or flat out having a very bad reputation. We prefer not to talk about what we will have almost no positive opinion, and although there are some that are in Beta phase, we prefer to wait for them to finish establishing themselves in the market before passing judgment, because as we said at the beginning of this chapter, the intention here is to help you make a proper choice about where to store your Bitcoin.

Now we will continue with desktop wallets, also known as offline software wallets. These are recommended for those who want some independence from the internet and its weaknesses. Having your Bitcoin stored in these types of cold wallets means that when a connection goes down, you can still keep your assets, but it also has its particular disadvantages that can vary from company to company. Therefore, here are the most interesting, the most popular ones, so that in some way we can make it easier for you to make a decision.

Exodus is the company that we like to say is ideal for visual people who love numbers. This application offers you extensive and detailed information through graphs, so you will not only be able to store your Bitcoin in it, but it will also show you the values and everything you need to know, in a very dynamic and visual way that all technology lovers can love.

On the other hand, it is important to mention that not only allows you to store Bitcoin, but you can also store in it other types of Cryptocurrencies, including Ethereum and Litecoin, among others. All for free through systems that can perfectly operate with Linux, Mac and Windows.

Draw your own conclusions, but from our trench we can tell you this is very complete, plus it does not generate any expense and gives you a lot of security and projection to both you and your savings in Cryptocurrencies.

ELECTRUM

Is the fastest among the private wallets. It has no major elements that differentiate it from other applications, except that its interface is really fast and allows you to make transactions directly with other users almost in record time. If you have no patience at all when moving your Bitcoins or simply want speed, this application is for you, in addition to obvious features such as being very safe. Like most of its kind.

JAXX LIBERTY

It is a very different wallet from the others because it does not want you to keep it. The service offered by this app is quite particular, it allows you to keep control of your data and the Bitcoins you have stored, but in such a broad way that you can use them to store them in any other wallet, at the same time it also gives you the option to convert one cryptocurrency to another, such as passing Bitcoin to Ethereum. We like to say that this is a pretty generous app that is worth taking into account in addition to being obviously quite secure and reliable.

. . .

MYCELLIUM

It is one of the safest, one of the best that exist, at the same time it is very advanced, with options of the highest level at the forefront of new technologies. The detail with this application is that it is only compatible with smartphones, only supports Bitcoin, and if you are an inexperienced or novice user, you may find it a bit complicated because it really is for connoisseurs who can take advantage of all its technological benefits.

BREAD WALLET

It is one of the most secure mobile wallets and at the same time one of the easiest to use. At first it was only available for iOS, but now it is also available for Android. According to the users themselves, there is no wallet for cell phones that is easier and simpler to use than this one. Its functions are basic, don't expect anything very technological or brilliant, but for beginners it's perfect.

COPAY

It is a wallet that offers you a unique function: create common funds where you can share your Bitcoin with friends, family or even partners, if you wish. This wallet has the particularity, moreover, that if you like you can manage more than one account, having for example, a person and a commercial one. When it comes to shared funds, you can create a group where all members must give approval before you issue the sending of crypto assets, so it is ideal, as we said, for partners, family or friends who share Bitcoin accounts and other Cryptocurrencies.

HARD WALLETS the best way to securely and reliably store your Cryptocurrencies

Now let's go to Hardware wallets. These are, without a doubt, the safest when it comes to combating electronic crimes. It is true that it is a physical device that can be lost or stolen, and you would still be exposed to lose all your Cryptocurrencies. But the truth is that this is very unlikely, unless you are a very careless person, very careless with your things.

Just by connecting the external memory or pen drive where this wallet is, you will be able to use it, and many of them you can even connect it to online wallets to do what in terms of Cryptocurrencies we call: pass crypto assets from cold to hot.

Without discussion this is the safest modality that exists in these times where the most egregious thefts are electronic, so here are two very specific options, which we consider the best on the market, if you want to buy a wallet of this style:

Trezor

It is, of all those of this style, the one that has been on the market for the longest time, which gives it a great reputation for staying active and full of followers in a world of transactions where most opt for hot modalities, that is, wallets or online wallets. Its price is close to $100 and it is not exactly the most modern, but it is very easy to access, quite simple to use, and it is undoubtedly the safest wallet of this and all types that may exist.

YOU CAN BUY HERE **the most modern TREZOR MODEL T:**

Or maybe you are interested in the TREZOR MODEL ONE:

Ledger nano S

In addition to being a little cheaper (less than $ 80) has a variety of very innovative features ranging from being able to enable and disable the pin to connect with almost all cryptocurrencies that exist, so it is not only useful for those who handle Bitcoin but also serves for those who are doing transactions with Ethereum, Litecoin and even altcoins. It is truly a modern marvel that provides almost armored security everywhere you look. You can buy it here:

SEE THE LEDGER NANO S HERE:

Finally, it is time to talk about paper wallets, the famous paper wallets. These are not as durable and resistant as the other physical version, the ones we have just shown you, but they are still very safe. You can keep them as a card, even give them as homemade gift cards if you want to give them as a gift, and you have a very practical facility when it comes to keeping them, which at the same time we can say that it is their curse.

Yes, you read that right. As we told you at the beginning of this explanation, paper wallets are very weak for the function they are going to fulfill, or so it seems to us, so we recommend that you keep them very well stored, even covered against water and anything else that can accelerate their deterioration.

They also have the difficulty that programming them is not exactly simple, and if you lose them, there is no way to recover them. Therefore, although they are practical and safe, they can be a double-edged sword. However, here are what we consider to be the two best paper wallets on the market if you want to use this option to store your Bitcoins.

BITADDRESS

It is perhaps the least indicated option if you are not a person very given to this kind of thing. It does not offer too much information except for a small tutorial on how to set it up, and although there are users who say that it is very easy to use, we also see that most have had to resort to YouTube tutorials once they have purchased it, because it was not very clear to them how to use it.

BitcoinPapperWallet

This is preferable to the previous one, if you ask us. It has a help center where you can consult any doubt or difficulty you present, and you can have the physical one in no time. It is free and you would only have to pay if you want to add or make use of certain options that are not technologically advanced such as holograms and counterfeit checking programs.

Having shown you all these options, we believe that at this point in the book, in this very chapter, it would be ideal to offer you what are our top 3 tips before you have to make a decision. As we have stated repeatedly throughout this book, our goal is to provide you with as much information as possible so that you can make the best decision now that you are about to enter the Bitcoin world.

Cover your back

Making backups, or what we IT call "Back up" can prove invaluable. It is an extra measure that can be useful when you least expect it but need it the most. You can use a device just for that, and you can keep it updated to avoid major problems.

Choose the option that best suits your needs

That includes taking into account your limitations. If you are a person who is just starting out in this, you may not want to use the most technologically advanced options for now because you could complicate the picture yourself. With this we do not want to tell you to limit yourself, you can dedicate yourself to learn more and more about Bitcoin, visit forums, download newsletters, keep yourself informed on social networks following crypto assets accounts and technological advances, so that later, when you have more experience, you can really take advantage of the software that attracts you the most.

Educate yourself

That goes hand in hand with what we advised you in the previous recommendation. If you keep reading, you can keep yourself updated, and as long as you are up to date with knowledge, you will be able to make better use of all the technology, get the most out of everything, and avoid risks as much as possible.

We could add many more recommendations, but for now, we prefer the rest to be a learning process that you will discover and build upon after the information we try to put at your service in this book.

So, go ahead, ready for the next chapter?

6

HOW TO GET BITCOINS FOR FREE

Want to get Bitcoins but don't have the money to buy them? Don't worry, this chapter is for you.

L et's start by saying that there is no such thing as free, or so we have learned in the business world, because that's what business is all about, giving something to get something in return, otherwise it wouldn't be called business and we would be talking about charity or things like that. Yes, you can get Bitcoins without paying, it is a reality. But you will still have to do something in return. If you are someone who wants to get Bitcoins but you don't have the capital to start, this chapter will be interesting for you because we will show you the different ways in which you can get the most famous and valuable cryptocurrency in the market, in exchange for a few hours of your time in activities that we are sure will not represent a great effort on your part.

From this moment on we will show you the 3 specific ways in which you can get Bitcoins without investing a penny, and at the same time, we will tell you about the different websites where you can accomplish each of these 3 different tasks, so you can choose for yourself which one to start with.

. . .

WE WON'T LIE to you, it is not a magic formula to have 100 Bitcoins in a week, if you read once a similar ad, we can guarantee that it is some kind of scam. But with perseverance, dedication and patience, you can get some Bitcoins in less time than it would take you to raise the money to buy them.

Mining Bitcoins

We're sure you've already read or heard about Bitcoin mining. It's not a myth, it's not fake, but it does have some specific requirements. We are not going to delve too much into this way of obtaining Bitcoins because it is so complex that we have decided to develop a whole chapter that you can find later in this book, with all the keys to be able to mine Bitcoins in an effective way.

However, we advance you that mining Bitcoins is really possible. Every day there are more and more people working at it and they have done very well. The problem with mining Bitcoins is that although it is true that you will not pay a penny for the Bitcoins you get by this means, you still have to invest in a quality, updated computer, a software that does the job and an electric energy fee that can be a bit high.

Yes, broadly speaking, mining Bitcoin is nothing more than programming a computer with a specific program to do the work for us. But as you have already seen, you need to invest in equipment, software, programs, and a lot of electricity. If this interests you, keep reading this book and later on you will have a very detailed chapter on how to achieve this quickly and easily. For now, let's move on to other points on how to get Bitcoins without spending a single cent.

WRITE About Bitcoins

. . .

THIS IS MORE FOR EXPERTS, people who are up to date in the market, who know how much a Bitcoin is worth, who can give recommendations on very specialized things such as giving a review on a specific storage software, making reviews on wallets or wallets, giving opinions on Cryptocurrency exchange platforms, among many other things you can write about Bitcoins.

You won't believe it, but there are numerous websites on the Internet that pay with Bitcoin if you write an article on a specialized topic about Bitcoins or even Cryptocurrencies in general. But remember, this is not for everyone. It is free, you do not have to invest any money, on the contrary, it is those sites that can pay you up to $100 in Bitcoin in exchange for a quality article. The detail is that, you must master the subject very well, have the ability to write a unique, original article, something that few people know, something that not everyone can write. We don't want to discourage you, but if you don't master the Bitcoin world too well, writing about it may not be for you.

However, if you think you do have the knowledge and literary quality to write interesting articles about Bitcoin, just go to any specialized website and send them an email with a sample of an article you can write, something you have already written, something totally original and interesting, and we guarantee that if it is good enough, they will at least respond, either to hire you, or at least recommend you or refer you to some other website of another colleague who they think might be interested in your services.

Now, if this is not your case, don't waste too much time on it. But do not worry that this is getting good, because the more we discard options, the closer we get to the one we have thought for you from the beginning, the one where you only need some time and patience to get Bitcoins without spending a single penny.

Have fun on sites that pay you with Bitcoin

This is the task you were waiting for; it is about entering websites where what you have to do is watch ads, watch videos, perform simple and even fun tasks such as playing in different activities, creating characters, among many other things.

The type of tasks or games is very varied, and below we will show you the most famous pages in which users themselves attest to having obtained Bitcoin in exchange for spending a few hours of their days dedicated to having fun or entertaining themselves on them.

FarmBitcoin is a website with typical farm games, like the one you probably played or watched on Facebook. It is about creating and growing a farm, cultivating, maintaining activity on the web, and after a while you will receive as payment for your time invested, fractions of Bitcoin. You won't get rich in a day, you won't have 100 Bitcoins in a week, but we assure you that for not having invested a penny and just playing, it is a wonderful way to start generating this famous and valuable cryptocurrency.

BTCCLICK

IT IS a great place to get Bitcoin in exchange for keeping clicking on the different pages that will be suggested to you while you are dedicated to them. By just clicking and looking at ads, among some other fairly simple tasks, you can earn Bitcoin in a really extremely simple way. Plus they have a very good reputation. There is no user who complains about not getting paid as promised.

Weekend Bitcoin

. . .

IT IS a page that its own name says it, you can make Bitcoin especially on weekends when things get even better. You get paid through Satoshis, which can range from a thousand per hour to 10.00 on weekends. what are you waiting for? All you have to do is log in and have fun.

Robotcoin

IT IS perfect if you are attracted to games with friendly and fun Robots. At the beginning it's a bit difficult, but as you play, you get the hang of it, complete the tasks, and you can earn up to 2,000 Satoshis in just one hour. We don't think it's a bad thing, huh?

MOONBITCOIN

IT'S one of the newest out there, and unlike most sites of this style, if for some reason you let several days go by without logging in, you'll see that once you pick it up again, the payout goes up. Maybe it is due to some reward policy that we do not understand, but we know first-hand that the users themselves are fascinated with it. We recommend that you join as soon as possible if you want to take advantage of it, because the few platforms with that nature, usually end up reaching a number of users very quickly and then do not admit new members. We are not saying that this is exactly what is going to happen, we do not want to play Nostradamus, we just tell you what we have seen with other sites as good as this one, and since this one is just starting, we recommend it immediately, especially because its users attest that they do pay.

FreeBitco.in

. . .

IT IS AN INTERESTING PLATFORM; it has a great reputation and all its users recommend it. It's all about entering codes and earning through chance. Then, when you have already collected a specific amount, you can participate in games where you can double or triple your winnings. It is true that in these games you can also lose everything you have won (Gambling), but it is not mandatory. You can perfectly keep playing and increase your winnings without risking anything. If you are interested in being able to start earning free Bitcoins you can start here:

BitcoinZebra

LIKE THE PREVIOUS EXAMPLE, it is a page where you perform a task to get Bitcoin, and then you can try to multiply your winnings in other games within the same page. The difference is that here it is about feeding a zebra, and with the winnings, you can go play dice. But the best thing is that if you lose at dice, you do not lose your winnings, the only thing you will have lost is the time invested, but what you have won is yours and no one will take it away from you. It is one of the most recommended when it comes to online games.

BITCOINKER

. . .

IT IS A SLIGHTLY MORE complex page, some users have not had patience for it, but the truth is that you only need to spend some time and you will see that the earnings will be real, much higher than those of the previous examples. Basically, it is a matter of solving captchas, giving your wallet data, and cashing out. As simple as that, but you don't get paid immediately but the first days of each month. Maybe that's why there are many users who don't have patience for it.

CRACKFAUCET

IT IS the opposite of the previous one and you can claim your Satoshis every 20 minutes. It also has a referral program where you can earn something extra by inviting other people to join and participate in the page, and if that were not enough, it has its own blog where it provides you with valuable and constant information about the Bitcoin, so you are up to date and know what to invest in, because we know that if you are reading this book is because you want to earn Bitcoin to enter the world of the Cryptocurrency business. Right?

FREEBITCOIN

IT'S for those people who like to push their luck. Without investing a single cent, you play a roulette where you can win Bitcoin, and the most interesting thing is that the page itself operates as a bank where you can keep your earnings generating an interest that exceeds 4%. We think it's a marvel, except for the detail that multiplying your earnings does not depend entirely on you, but largely on luck. But come on, not bad for not having invested a single cent. Start earning free Bitcoins here:

SwissAdsPaysFaucet

IT IS VERY similar to the previous one, it is about online gambling, but it gives you many more options. It also offers you the opportunity to save and generate 4% interest, but if you invest a little on the site you get even more gambling options. We don't recommend the latter, especially since we have written this chapter of the book dedicated to people who don't have money to invest in Bitcoin, but we feel the obligation to mention it because it is what has given them the most fame. Most of their users recommend it because they consider that small investment worth it for even bigger gains.

BONUS BITCOIN

It is a page that enamors anyone through what they offer in their own name: bonuses. It's all about highlighting yourself in any of their three options, either by performing tasks, watching ads or participating in games of chance. The interesting thing is that it offers you a high amount of bonuses in which you can even double your earnings. They give you bonuses for productivity, for perseverance, for remaining active, and even for preferring them and recommending them to friends who end up registering on the page. We think it is perfect for that reason, because the more time you dedicate to them, the more you help them to become famous, the greater the benefit will be.

. . .

ClaimBtc

It is one of the most famous nowadays, although most of its users complain that it is plagued with ads and publicity. If you want to work on it, it is very easy to get Bitcoin solving Captchas, but be careful not to waste too much time on advertising that does not generate profits or in the worst case acquire a virus.

Now, if your thing is to watch videos on ads only, here are 4 specific examples, the most famous and recommended pages where the only thing you have to do is watch videos and get paid for it.

BtcVic

It is a page where in just seconds you can make several Satoshis, but if you want to withdraw low amounts, they charge commissions of up to 2%. Ideally, you should let your earnings accumulate until you reach a certain amount so that you do not lose so much in commissions, plus you can earn much more, several extra Satoshis by referring friends. In fact, just by registering you get a bonus of 50 Satoshis. That is why it is one of the most recommended.

BTC Clicks

It is similar to the previous one, you can earn up to 4 Satoshis for watching videos of just 20 seconds and you can earn an extra commission if you make your friends participate in it. The bad thing is that if you let a month and a half pass without activity in your account, they withdraw everything, absolutely everything you have earned, plus you cannot make withdrawals until you have already generated a considerable amount of Satoshis.

Coin Bulb is similar to the previous ones, but a little more rigorous when registering. It requires you to confirm by email and they don't give you bonuses for registering. But you can earn up to 60% for your referred friends, and if you pay the Premium version, you can earn up to 100% of what your friends earn. Once again, we tell you that we do not like to recommend sites to earn Bitcoin for free where then give you options where you also spend, but also, once again this is one of the options that have liked the most to their own users, so we feel obliged to comment.

Bitter.io

It is similar to the previous ones but the earnings can be double. The detail is that it is a little more complex to start with, not only does it ask you for several data to register, but you will also have to download some things to be able to use the page as it should be. Many users recommend it for being very little invasive, that is, it has very few advertisements, so you can dedicate yourself to generate Bitcoins in a pleasant and quiet way.

Now that we have shown you the options you have to watch videos and perform entertaining and fun tasks very similar to games, it is time to show you what the real games are, the ones that are video games, those with real interaction and very dynamic.

Tomy Game

It is a video game that will remind you of those classic Tom and Jerry cartoons. You can win up to almost 100 Satoshis per day and you can participate in races against other users, where the winner gets to keep the other's winnings. It is a very interactive game where as you progress you unlock other mini-games in which you can keep winning fractions of Bitcoin. It is wonderful and entertaining, a real way to win by playing.

BitFun

IT IS a page like no other because there is no other that surpasses it in the more than 600 games it has, all very varied, and in which you can win Bitcoins. You read that right, more than 600 different games. You can spend a whole day just looking at the options, although that is not our recommendation. The fact is that it is great for the variety offered, it will be almost impossible to get bored of winning Bitcoin on this page, in addition to offers already known as winning a percentage for the friends you get to sign up and participate in this page.

Well, as well as these that we mentioned, there are many others, you can investigate for yourself. We only want to show you the most popular ones that also have a very good reputation and are recommended by their own users. Once again, we admit that it will not be much Bitcoin that you can generate from these options, but we think it is a wonderful way to start if you do not have money to invest. Once you have already earned a little, you can go to the serious market and multiply your earnings in other ways that we will explain later in this book.

7

BITCOIN TRADING

In the previous chapters we have shown you how to get Bitcoin, in fact we started by explaining the basics, we even told you how it came about, whose idea it was to create Bitcoin, how it is used and what it was created for. We were also kind enough to show you even curious facts, anecdotes of people who became rich and famous overnight by investing in Bitcoin. We have also shown you that Bitcoin is not the only cryptocurrency on the market, only that the others that exist still do not surpass the first one, which we consider the best of all, the Bitcoin.

In this chapter, since we have taught you how to get Bitcoin, and how to store them safely, it is time to talk about everything you can do with it, and definitely the most interesting thing to do with Bitcoin in a way that will generate profits, is to do what is known as Trading, which is nothing more than buying and selling taking advantage of the benefits of a fluctuating market, which is always going up and down and therefore, if you are avid enough, you can make the most of it.

First of all, we must explain what Bitcoin trading is. Bitcoin trading is nothing more than buying and selling Bitcoins, as simple as that. It is done with the intention of buying the lowest price and then selling it at the highest price. It is the same thing that happens with the dollar in Latin America, for example. With the difference that the Bitcoin is a currency controlled by no government or any institution. In fact, that is the reason why the Bitcoin is currently, and has always been, the best cryptocurrency on the market. There is an absolute guarantee that nobody controls it, only the market itself, and we know that the market in general is not something that one person, much less one institution can control.

Now, there are many platforms, many pages where you can buy and sell. Below we will give you our best reviews of what we believe are the most popular sites for Bitcoin trading, and we will also tell you our impressions, so that now that you know everything about Bitcoin, you can choose the option that best suits your tastes and interests and you can sell your Bitcoins at the best price.

BINANCE

IT IS BASED IN CHINA, is one of the most famous so far, one of the most renowned worldwide. Although it is relatively new, it is one of the most preferred by most people. It only charges something like 0.1% commissions if you are just starting out, but those commissions can be increased if you want to make use of all its technological goodness. We think it is one of the favorites because you will hardly find another one as advanced as this one. It is a platform to buy and sell almost any type of cryptocurrency, although we know that the most popular is the Bitcoin, however, so far there is no cryptocurrency already established in the market that you can't buy or sell within this platform.

You can get started and register here:

This platform is also one of the most innovative in other ways, it offers you a wide security, which has also given it a lot of fame for people who want to trade high amounts of Bitcoin. In other words, if you are already an expert you can go for this option, but if you are a beginner who aspires to learn a lot and go far, that is, if you are someone ambitious who aspires to trade very soon to very high denominations, we can also recommend it with eyes closed as most of its users do.

Bittrex

BITTREX IS another established platform that has been operating for almost half a decade in the United States. It has a reputation for being the only platform that focuses on achieving a particular goal, to be fully up to date with the laws worldwide. There is no platform in the whole world that is not as up to date with the law, which makes it one of the safest platforms on which to trade. On the other hand, it is also known that this platform allows trading almost 200 different types of cryptocurrencies, which makes it quite attractive for all markets, because remember that although the Bitcoin is the most famous worldwide there are countries where they operate with other types of cryptocurrencies, while it is also very interesting for those creators of cryptocurrencies that are just launching their brand to the market. Perhaps because of its eagerness to be the most legal platform, it is precisely because many Cryptocurrency brands, especially the new ones, are very interested in registering in this space that provides total security since 2014.

POLONIEX

LIKE THE PREVIOUS PLATFORM, it has been operating since 2014. This platform has the reputation, not only of being one of the safest, as they have never reported any type of theft or fraud, just like the majority that we bring you today as a recommendation in this article, but also charges one of the lowest commissions in the market, being between 0.15 and 0.25%, and is one of the most famous for new alternative Cryptocurrency brands. That is, it is not like the previous one, it does not host all types of cryptocurrencies, but it does host most of those that try to compete with Bitcoin.

KUCOIN

IT IS another platform preferred by many because it offers various types of bonuses in addition to its commission is very low. There are stocks for which it charges nothing at all, and others for which it charges just 0.1%. It also boasts of being one of the most innovative, offering a series of advantages to its users that if we were to detail them, we would have to make a separate chapter just to explain them. Perhaps it is not necessarily the best for beginners, not because it is difficult to use, on the contrary, it is one of the easiest to handle and where you can trade your Bitcoins faster, what happens is that it offers so many alternatives for experts, that if you are not one, you would be wasting all the good that this platform has to offer.

. . .

CRYPTOPIA

IT IS A VERY broad platform that to those starting out on it seems like a kind of complex and confusing wilderness. However, many users confess that the more they use it, the more they understand it. It is complex, offers many functions, and accepts the most different cryptocurrencies. The number of cryptocurrencies that you can buy or sell there is so absurd that it exceeds 400, almost reaching 500, and every day there are more and more different cryptocurrencies that you can trade on this platform. In addition to that, it can compete perfectly in the market because it has a very low commission of 0.20%, and if that were not enough, it only asks you for an email so you can register, so trading on it is very basic and simple. Most of its users are from Europe, they are based in New Zealand, but they have been expanding their market worldwide and today they have users from all over the world.

Bitfinex

IT IS another one of those platforms that should almost have the seal of being only for experts. Currently you cannot create a new account on it, and if you are an inexperienced user, there is really no room for you on it. However, as we always want you to be as well informed as possible, we mention and detail it. Like most of the platforms where high denomination trades are made, the commissions are very low. They do not exceed 0.20% in commissions, but this is because there is not a single platform in the world that exceeds them in terms of Bitcoin trading. At the time of writing this chapter had already been made trading millions and millions of dollars in Bitcoin, and is closed to new members unless you sign up on a waiting list where you will be called by your trading experience and your economic capacity. We know it sounds a bit or quite elitist but the truth is that it has what it takes, they are the most renowned platform when it comes to Bitcoin trading, plus they offer very exclusive security systems only for experts. As we said at the beginning, we know it is not for you right now, but who knows if later you become an expert and they even ask you to join their platform. Do not discard them, learn every day a little more and you will surely become the same or even more expert than the common and frequent users of this platform.

Kraken

It is one of the safest and most reliable of those operating in the United States. They have the advantage of being a platform based in San Francisco although for some reason they do not operate in New York. Outside of New York, they not only operate in all other states but also control a large part of the European market and have also managed to reach Canada. They offer interesting benefits in that the higher your transactions, the lower the commissions you will be charged. It is of that type of platforms for experienced, it is known that they are the one that sells or buys more Bitcoin in the middle of Euros, and it is also known that they only do trading of Cryptocurrencies, including many others that are not only Bitcoin, but it is also a platform to buy Euros or dollars if that is what you are looking for. They also have the reputation of being one of the safest because it offers a double authentication system before you start using your account, ie from the login, and also has a second security system that is amplified as you go using your account and making your operations.

Huobi

. . .

IT IS the most technological of all Asian platforms, They operate from China for several years, are very innovative and offers its users many interesting graphics that are very useful, which are provided by tradingview, so it is a perfect platform for trading on a large scale, something like the others that we have told you that are mostly for experts, only this in turn, besides being very safe and innovative, is quite visual and attractive for those who need to be constantly monitoring the numbers when making their transactions. On the other hand, we can and we must tell you that it is perhaps the only one that is really shielded against almost all types of cyber-attacks, so it is preferred by those who have a high sense of security, recommended for those who believe that safeguarding their money in the best possible way is something far beyond paranoia.

Okex

IT IS the platform with the lowest commission in the market, no one will beat them in that, ever. We know that the normal average is between 0.20 and 0.30 5, but this platform charges just 0.03%, something that seems absurd, but it is as true as the fact that they are a very safe platform. To many users, especially to the most expert and new, or used to technology and its benefits, it seems strange to use a desktop platform, but this type of software can be interesting when talking about security, they are easy to install, do not take too much time, and are an alternative if you want to try something different that will really be much cheaper than the rest, that is to say, than the competition.

LIQUI

.   .   .

FOR ITS PART is an Exchange platform where you can not only buy and sell your Bitcoins but other types of Cryptocurrencies, with the interesting feature that you can also open a savings account in which you will generate 24% annual interest. That high number aroused our curiosity, so we consulted with several users and it turned out that it was true, no one has complained of fraud or scam in that sense, so we could recommend, however, we also learned that they are a platform that is not regulated, so many people might distrust, but the truth is that no other trading platform or Exchange, are regulated, and remember that precisely therein lies the particular and interesting both Bitcoin and the rest of the Cryptocurrency in general that are not controlled by any agency or any government.

Bitmex

IT IS an Exchange platform that we could not leave out because in addition to offering trading services as all the previous ones.

You can also make interesting bets on whether the Bitcoin will go up or down. That is, it is like playing the stock market. You win if you invest in a currency whose value rises, but at the same time it is a casino type betting house in which if you manage to predict and get it right in that sense, you can double and even triple your earnings, according to how much you bet.

Now, within this type of this page there is a thing called leverage, which can be very risky when investing in Bitcoin or any other cryptocurrency. But on the other hand, we must inform you that leverage is nothing more than a kind of financial aid, that is, leverage is when an investor wants to increase his capital and he does it through a loan which is made by the Exchange, but he does not do it for free, but obviously charges a commission for it.

The disadvantages of leverage, is that you can ask or request that loan trusting that the cryptocurrency in which you are going to invest, will go up in value. If you ask for that loan and the opposite happens, you will still have to repay that loan in the agreed time, so it is a big risk. This is not something that we recommend for the moment if you are a beginner, but once you are familiar with all this and if you are probably fully dedicated to trading Bitcoin or any other cryptocurrency in general, we recommend you do it because it certainly has benefits, but we also warn you that you should be extremely cautious and be aware of the consequences that can have the flow of the market in this type of phenomena.

We should also tell you about scalping as a trading method or strategy. This is something that you can do using in an agile and ingenious way the data that tradingview offers you.

Tradingview is a free website that offers you a look at the market, there you can know the value of each asset, among them can reflect the price of Bitcoin in dollars. If you are constantly monitoring the Bitcoin on that page, you will know when it has started to go down, which indicates that this is the right time to start buying, but you should only do it for a very short term, as indicated by the scalping strategy, which is about that, to buy at the best price for a very short time, and then start selling, also for a short time, while the asset keeps rising, even some experts recommend that it should not be done while it is rising, but when we have observed that it has reached its highest point, that we know that it will not overcome so easily and that indicates that it is close to the time to start going down.

In this way, we believe that we have made it quite clear that there are many platforms for trading, all very varied, very different from each other, and that we have made available to you all the information you need to start trading. You already know how to get Bitcoin, you already know the places to choose a place to store it, and you even know how to buy more and then sell it, playing with its value in the market. We think it's time to take the next step, which we have prepared for you in the next chapter.

8

BITCOIN MINING WHAT IS IT ALL ABOUT?

As we have already explained almost all the ways to make Bitcoin transactions, it is time to tell you about the only one where you don't have to pay for Bitcoin but you don't have to do any work to get them. It will seem very strange to you, but it turns out that you can, it is possible to get Bitcoin without buying them and without making an effort to have them, letting computers and specialized programs do it for you.

In order for you to understand this in a simple way, it is important to remember what we told you in the first chapters where we talked about the importance of Bitcoin transactions and blockchains. Remember that blockchains are like a kind of ledger where all the transactions that people make from one to another in buying and selling Bitcoin are recorded. Well, it turns out that those transactions use a Hash number that is very important, which is what is known as the hash rate when mining Bitcoin.

WHAT BITCOIN MINING does is to decipher the algorithms until it finds those hashes that are very valuable and important, that's where the importance of the hash rate going up lies, because the higher it goes up, the more value it has.

It turns out that the mysterious creator of the Bitcoin, somehow and to use a term that allows this explanation to be more graphic and easier to understand, hid or buried 21 million Bitcoins in the network. Those 21 million Bitcoins can come to public light if they are mined, that is, discovered by miners. It turns out that it is not necessarily that you will find them, but that if you manage to mine and solve the corresponding algorithms, you can win some of those Bitcoins as a prize for having contributed to the construction of the blockchain.

To make a long story short, there are ways in which you can mine those Bitcoins and earn them without breaking a sweat.

How do you do that?

WELL, first you must have a set of equipment suitable for that, remembering that the more equipment you have, the more opportunities you will have to mine Bitcoin. On the other hand, it is important for you to know that it is not enough to have equipment suitable for it, but you will also need to have the programs that are for it. That way, having the computers and the programs to mine Bitcoin, what you will need is to have a good internet, a room with a suitable temperature so that the equipment does not overheat, and a stable electrical system that does not fail and that you are willing to pay, because several computers mining Bitcoins at the same time is something that will consume a lot of electricity and the bill can be a little high.

Having all these specifications that we have pointed out above, you will understand that you do not need to lift a finger to mine Bitcoin because the technology and services will do all the work for you.

. . .

BELOW YOU WILL FIND information about the most interesting equipment you can buy to mine Bitcoin, as well as the best programs to do it, in case you decide to enter the wonderful and interesting world of Bitcoin mining.

Avalon6

IT IS PERHAPS the one with the most power, therefore many users recommend it. It is not only the strongest but also has a very interesting speed range compared to the other two options that we will mention after this one. However, paradoxically, it is the one with the lowest capacity, that is to say, it has a lot of strength but you will not be able to mine too much with just one of these machines. In fact, in reality, a single piece of equipment, whatever it is, won't do you much good. Ideally, you should be able to run several at the same time. With this one, unlike others, you will not be able to mine more Bitcoin but you will be able to do it in less time.

AntminerS7

IT IS a computer with less power but with much more capacity, so mining with it can be slower, but at the same time you can reach interesting levels of Bitcoin mining.

AntminerS9

IT IS perfect if you want to increase your Bitcoin mining capacity to very high levels. It is something like the previous one but in an improved version ready to test your limits.

Now, it's time to tell you about what we think are the best programs to mine Bitcoin, so that if you have already purchased your computer for it, you only have to choose one of these options and you can start mining your own Bitcoin without sweating a single drop.

MINER GATE IS perfect for beginners, according to its users and even its own creators, especially because it has very simple instructions for use, easy to program, and has intelligent functions in which it not only mines but also selects the cryptocurrency, because in addition to Bitcoin, with it you can mine Dash, Ethereum, among others.

CG miner is one of the most recommended by experts, it has interesting functions, is compatible with almost all operating systems and very useful when it comes to leaving the computer doing everything for you. One of the disadvantages is that since it does not have a background window, it can be a bit complicated to use if you are not an expert.

50 MINER IS PERHAPS the most interesting among those that have the rare feature of being several in one. That is, it offers you different programs and you choose which one to use depending on the currency you are mining or the characteristics of mining, including your goals and intentions.

DIABLO MINER IS a program that can scare you more than its name. It really is very advanced, it is compatible with the most advanced graphics cards, that is, it is perfect for mining Bitcoin at the highest level, but if you do not have years of experience in this, it will rather be a waste of money and time for you because you will find it confusing and even a little stressful.

Awesome miner is our last software on the list, it is the only one that only works with Windows, at least of the ones we are able to recommend. It has an interesting remote-control feature, which allows you to monitor it remotely without having to worry too much about not being near it.

Now that you know all the basics of mining, you can start mining. There are no more excuses, at least not in knowledge. Now you only have to invest some money in equipment and then program it, because the truth is that you will not have to make too much effort or spend too much time, because the wonderful thing about mining Bitcoin is that the equipment and programs do everything for you.

9

ALTCOINS AND WHICH ONES CAN MAKE YOU WEALTHY

We have already explained in all the previous chapters what Bitcoin is all about. We have provided you with everything you need to know to understand the Bitcoin, from how to have it, to how to store it, including very important details about how to acquire it, which are the best platforms for trading, and a whole series of knowledge that is very important and that you need when making transactions with this famous cryptocurrency.

Now, the existence of Bitcoin in the market, and all the phenomenon it has generated as a cryptocurrency, has caused a great interest in new cryptocurrencies. Bitcoin was the first one, the spearhead, the first one that came to the market back in 2009, almost a decade ago. Now, all the other almost a thousand different cryptocurrencies that exist, have emerged following in the footsteps of the pioneer in this world of cryptocurrencies.

The interesting thing about this, and perhaps what has caused all this boom, is that Bitcoin is a reality, it is not a fraud, much less a thing pulled by the hair. Bitcoin is here to stay, and the ultimate proof is not so much the high value it has acquired in the market compared to the dollar as perhaps the most important currency worldwide, but that it has even become a very well-established means of payment.

Altcoins are nothing more than alternative currencies, other currencies that have emerged in the hope of matching or even surpassing Bitcoin. This is wonderful because it legitimizes the market and further drives home the importance of Bitcoin. At first it was believed that Bitcoin could be a kind of fraud, a trap to dominate the market, to monopolize everything that is about Cryptocurrencies, but precisely its freedom in the market is what has led to the existence of others such as those already known today, including Litecoin, Ethereum, Dash, and many others more So as these Cryptocurrencies emerge hoping to become something like Bitcoin, more and more people are interested in these new Cryptocurrencies to see if they run with the same fate of the early adopters of Bitcoin. In other words, their dream is to invest in a new, low-value cryptocurrency, which in a few years will skyrocket and be worth as much or more than the famous Bitcoin so that their lives will change and they can become millionaires.

Currently there are many altcoins, some even with such strange names that we dare not mention them, but there are also several that aim to skyrocket later on.

In this chapter we will try to show you everything you need to know about some of them, in case after becoming an expert in Bitcoin you decide to invest in one of them. As you know, since the first chapter we have told you that no other cryptocurrency has reached the levels of Bitcoin, but more and more computer geniuses are teaming up with experts in economics and marketing, and it is very likely that sooner rather than later a new cryptocurrency will emerge that will reach the same or even further.

In fact, there are already some altcoins that have gone quite far, such as Ethereum, for example. For now, however, it is very difficult for them to imitate the genius of the p2p payment system and blockchain.

We could dedicate an entire book to just tell you about all the altcoins that exist, but it would be pointless. Therefore, we will only tell you about the ones that apparently can make you a millionaire before the end of 2018, or at least it is believed that by 2019 their value will have shot up in an interesting way in the market.

MIOTA (Iota)

IT IS A NEW CRYPTOCURRENCY, one more altcoin, just like the rest of the ones we are going to detail in this chapter. This specific one was created in 2015 and is one of the most talked about, many of those who have invested in it so far are small companies of medium-sized entrepreneurs, and some technology operators are already using it as a means of payment.

The main reason that makes it an attractive altcoin is the fact that all transactions made on its unique blockchain, will be totally free, or at least for the moment they are. This makes it really attractive to the market, and thus it seems to be an interesting altcoin to invest in.

XRP (RIPPLE)

THIS IS an altcoin that has already started to skyrocket in value, only that so far it has not done so at a dizzying pace as Bitcoin already did at the time. However, we can tell you in 2017 it shot its value by almost 300%, so we think it is a good altcoin to invest in, at the same time we know that there are already more than 100 banks that have already adapted it to their blockchain.

0x (ZRX)

. . .

It is one of the newest altcoin, of which not too much is known, however we know that it exists since 2017 and that its crypto-assets were distributed among its partners and operational expenses, a large part, going to market just a little more than half.

What makes it a rather interesting altcoin, is that it combines the two modalities, i.e. the centralized part, and the decentralized part. It offers the best of both worlds, so we would not be surprised if in the coming months more and more people invest in it if they manage to develop a great campaign that catapults them into the market and makes them become established.

Golem (GNT)

This is another of the newest ones, relatively speaking. It has the great attraction of working in a decentralized way and seems to be a very good option for technological corporations, and it is said, for example, that it can serve as a payment currency for advanced issues of very large companies that need to pay for animation services, such as Pixar, among many other options.

It is known that so far it is a cryptocurrency or altcoin that has increased its value so far by 15%, which is not necessarily a very high number next to its peers, but there are several reasons to think that it is about to grow in the market.

As well as these four altcoins we have just described, there are about a thousand more cryptocurrencies. All trying to match Bitcoin or at least mimic its levels of success.

You already know the story of the early-adopters, of those people who invested early in Bitcoin when nobody knew that cryptocurrency, when almost everybody doubted, when almost everybody even believed that although it was not necessarily a fraud, at least it would be a failure, that it would not achieve everything that was said about it, but it turned out that its creator took things to a high level, and you see, the consequences cannot be called that way because it would sound catastrophic. It ends up being more convenient, fair and accurate, to call everything positive that Bitcoin has achieved results.

Investing in Altcoin for the remainder of 2018 can be an interesting way to start seeing gains for 2019, or perhaps a bit further down the road. If you want to invest in Altcoins you shouldn't do so expecting your shares to multiply and make you a millionaire overnight.

REMEMBER that those people who became rich investing in Bitcoin, managed to see the multiplication of their assets, several months or even up to years after having deposited their money and trust in Bitcoin. With these altcoins it will surely be the same, however, these four examples that we mention in this penultimate chapter, were selected in a studied way because according to the projections they are the altcoins that aim to shoot their value very soon in the market.

The proof that there are cryptocurrencies that can reach those values is that there are already some that have already done so, among them Ethereum, Litecoin, and one or another that is approaching interesting levels although they are still far away from Ethereum itself, and therefore not to mention the distance that separates them from Bitcoin.

IT MUST BE SAID, Bitcoin seems unreachable, it seems like a giant that is very difficult for any altcoin to reach. It is so much so, that thanks to the fact that Bitcoin is the established cryptocurrency par excellence, besides being the first, that is, they are pioneers in the market; they have created the phenomenon of having to create a new term for the other emerging cryptocurrencies and that is why this chapter and the whole world speaks of these other currencies as what they are, an alternative to what already exists.

Investing in Altcoin is, on the other hand, not something you should do lightly. For that we show you all these options, and we also clarify that there are many others. There have been counted up to more than 400 different Cryptocurrencies that you can buy within a single page. There are Exchange pages that are dedicated to trading only the most popular ones, but as we explained in previous chapters, there are those that handle almost all altcoins on the market. This is done with the intention that you have in each page, in each platform.

Just as in other chapters we showed you all the platforms for Bitcoin trading, in this chapter we intended to let you know just some of the options that the market offers you for this year and next year if you decide to invest in any altcoin. Remember that this way of investing in cryptocurrencies is something that can pay very good dividends in the long term when it comes to new altcoins, those that have not yet exploded but are supposed to do so.

IT IS true that there are hundreds of altcoins that have not yet done so and probably never will, which is why we have not spent too much effort in telling you about other altcoins that we don't even trust. And we don't trust them, not because we think they are frauds, although we don't have proof to the contrary either, but simply because they are not within the limelight of what experts in economics and tech corporations mention. You must not forget that all these altcoins are something really modern and point towards a new world in which cash will become obsolete, a thing of the past, an archaic source of trade and contributing to an economy that perhaps will come a time when it will no longer exist, because everything will have changed for the better, mutating towards new trends, more and more comfortable, better and better thought out even in terms of ecology.

When we say that altcoins, as well as Bitcoin itself, point to ecological issues, we say it because we know that the world is in decline, every time the felling of trees and the deterioration of the ozone layer is greater, so trading, making all kinds of payments and commercial transactions electronically, making paper money unnecessary, can be an alternative so that not only trade but many other important things in life end up moving to the 2. 0 and start once and for all a new era in which it is no longer necessary to print paper and therefore trees can grow and flourish in peace.

We do not want to sound like hippies, we do not want to be fanatical environmentalists, we are just mentioning just one of the benefits why altcoins and all cryptocurrencies in general, are much more than an alternative to Bitcoin. All these cryptocurrencies make or can make it unnecessary to print invoices, spend papers and papers, millions of them in accounting books and the like.

So, if in any way we can help to enlighten you when it comes to investing your money, we like and are very pleased that this is the case, and that you learn everything you need to know about Cryptocurrencies in general, but most especially about Bitcoin.

WE WOULD LIKE to close this chapter by reminding you of several things we have mentioned in other sections of this book:

CRYPTOCURRENCIES HAVE NOT ONLY COME to stay and Bitcoin is the proof of it, but they exist to establish themselves in a new market model, and the existence of so many alternatives as all those almost a thousand altcoins that operate since ay in the market and that aim to multiply day after day, are nothing more than evidence that the market needs to be free, the market wants to leave intermediaries and point to something else, to something different.

THE ALTCOINS ARE PROOF, not only that Bitcoin is right to bet on a new market, but also that it does not intend to take over the entire industry by itself, because there is a reason why the others can exist. The formula is there, they just need to know how to apply it so that we migrate once and for all to a new system, to a new market model in which banks will cease to be something so powerful, to become what they really should be, a service for which we pay only if we really want and need it, and finally understand that they are the ones who depend on us, and not vice versa as we have been led to believe all this time.

We want to clarify that we have nothing against the common and regular systems that already exist and have been operating for so long, but the altcoins represent a kind of cyber revolution that comes to rescue people from mistaken beliefs, from a world where there is no real freedom of business sometimes and where there are more and more risks of being victims of cyber-attacks and electronic theft.

IN THIS LAST sense we can say that altcoins are much more than an alternative to Bitcoin, they are a real alternative to the models already operating in the market that every day give us more arguments to want to do without them, and when it comes to that, altcoins represent much more than a simple option.

Now, while it is true that if you want to invest in cryptocurrencies to get rich like the early adopters of Bitcoin did, you should do so by investing in altcoins, in those cryptocurrencies that are just coming to market and that could multiply their value incredibly as Bitcoin has already done, in the next chapter we will talk about how and why Bitcoin is still an interesting alternative to invest despite having a very high value at the moment, and how that high value it has at this point may mean nothing with the one it will most likely reach in the days to come.

Don't miss the fascinating end of this book, there is still one more chapter to reveal how Bitcoin is still an alternative to make you a successful multi-millionaire.

10

WHY SHOULD YOU START NOW?

T hroughout the previous nine chapters we have shown you everything you need to know about Bitcoin and Cryptocurrencies in general, putting at your service a knowledge that we know can be as useful as enriching if you know how to use it for your own benefit and for the benefit of those around you, because the most important thing about knowledge is to know how to take advantage of it for positive things, things that can contribute to humanity, And we know that if you are a person who manages to invest your money wisely and manages to multiply it, surely you will also make great efforts to help others to reach where you have reached, so that every day there are more successful people and the world of Cryptocurrencies, which has come to stay, is just a bridge between the new era of technologies and the welfare of people.

Now that you not only know all about Bitcoin but also know that there are many other cryptocurrencies in which to invest, it is time to tell you why even though Bitcoin has a high value, it may be just a decimal of the value it can reach within the next ten years.

We are not going to lie to you, what we are going to explain in this chapter is a long-term issue, we will not talk to you, as we have not done in any chapter of this book, about becoming a millionaire overnight. What we have told you is that with things like trading and scalping in the world of buying and selling cryptocurrencies, you can invest one day and double and even triple your profits very quickly, and we have shown you with facts, with real examples, with formulas and strategies and how to buy and sell crypto assets on the best platforms where you can not only buy at good prices and sell at even more convenient prices, but we have also shown you a whole variety of sources to get profits through interest by keeping your Bitcoins or altcoins inside platforms that reward you for loyalty and even give you a percentage of their profits if you refer them to your friends and acquaintances, and that happens because that is how this business operates, this new world of virtual currencies free of intermediaries where all of us who participate can earn something, especially those who invest the money, because that is what Cryptocurrencies and the spaces where you can trade for them are aimed at, so that the real investors are the ones who have the power, so that those who worked to obtain those profits, are the ones who really see them reflected in their accounts and in their lifestyle, acquiring goods they need, goods they want, and giving their loved ones what they deserve and need.

Well, it turns out that in one of the previous chapters we told you that the Bitcoin aims to become extinct, it is limited, it is not like other regular currencies where a central bank or some agency prints as many bills as it takes. It turns out that Bitcoin are limited, there is only a specific amount that we have seen on the network, in addition to those that are already in the wallets or electronic wallets of those who already own them.

Remember something, you can trade Bitcoin with those that are already in someone's possession, including yourself, that is, those Bitcoins that are bought and sold like hot cakes on the platforms or even directly between users through the block chains that we have explained in detail in other chapters, but there is also an interesting amount that is buried in the network.

.   .   .

Do not forget that its creator, the genius who invented not only Bitcoin but all the ways to make secure transactions with it, buried or hid on the internet an amount that is said to be 21,000. 000 Bitcoin that still have no owner, and those are the Bitcoin that can be accessed through Bitcoin mining, that complex process of which we already explained much, and which in turn is so specialized that it cannot really be executed by the hand of man but you have to buy really smart computers to do the work of deciphering algorithms to get to have the power to discover and win those Bitcoins as a prize and win them and make them yours so you can then do with them what you want, including selling them, if you wish.

The interesting thing about this detail is that it is presumed that once all those Bitcoins are mined, there will be no more Bitcoins, that is, there will be no hope of obtaining them by other means than buying them. Some call it programmed obsolescence, the creator was smart enough to create something that knows that at some point it will run out, there will be no new Bitcoins, and the market and all the people who operate with Bitcoin will have no choice but to buy Bitcoin to those who have kept them saved during all this time that is estimated to be about a decade what it will take to discover through mining all those Bitcoin that still have no owner and are under the dirt of the internet, buried somewhere waiting to be discovered.

It is believed then that the current value of Bitcoin is nothing compared to what it will reach in about a decade, when there are no more new Bitcoins to be discovered and when Bitcoin is already so well established in the market that it will be impossible to do without it, so that somehow chaos will break out that will make corporations, especially the larger ones that work with it, have to run and resort to the big platforms, But not only to them to acquire new Bitcoins and thus not interrupt their operations, but even ordinary people who have kept Bitcoin during all that time, will have in their hands something very valuable, something almost in kind of extinction and we already know that scarce things that at the same time are very necessary, come to have a level of demand so great that its value soars in almost astronomical ways.

It is expected that for the next few years, the value of Bitcoin will continue to fall, as it has been doing so far, but all this obeys a natural and normal law of supply and demand. At the moment there is enough Bitcoin in the market and therefore its value may decrease, in fact, we are reaching a point where there are more and more Bitcoin than people needing it and that is because the boom in which people invested frantically in Bitcoin has passed, and therefore, there are times when there are more people selling than buying Bitcoin.

But as we tell you in previous paragraphs and as we have maintained throughout this book in all previous chapters, the Bitcoin is a currency that tends to fluctuate with the market, and just as at this moment its demand has dropped a little, we know that there will come a time when it will rise almost immeasurably, and therefore, if the supply fails to meet that demand, the value of the Bitcoin will not only skyrocket again, but reach levels never seen before and all the people who own Bitcoin will be able to declare themselves millionaires once they sell them because its value will rise in such a way that it will reach a price in the market too high and everyone who wants Bitcoin will have to pay it, and everyone who has Bitcoin will be able to charge a lot for those cryptoassets he owns and thus he will surely be able to solve his life and those of his future generations through a market depreciation in which he will get all the benefits of an interesting and complex economy that aims to be the best of the new world era.

Now, as we have told you throughout this book that we have written with dedication in order to offer you all the information you need to know about Bitcoin and altcoins and thus be able to make important decisions about your economy, the early-adopters (as the first people who dare to invest in a new product are called) of Cryptocurrencies today are millionaires thanks to Bitcoin. We are talking about people who invested very little money back in 2009 and today own a fortune.

Knowing that we have just reminded you, we wonder what would happen if we invest in Bitcoin and in ten years history repeats itself and those of us who have deposited our money in that cryptocurrency become wealthy multimillionaires who can also enter the industry in a powerful way, because the latter is a detail that we have not told you about so far.

Not only we can become multimillionaires thanks to having known how to invest in something that then increases its value in unexpected and at the same time very high ways, but we can also become an important part of that industry, because if we not only dedicate ourselves to save and sell, but we become great investors, important people in this whole world of Cryptocurrencies, and if we achieve all that, we can not only be millionaires but also important and famous people in the world economy.

In all the previous chapters we have dedicated some words to remind you the importance of knowledge, and in this chapter, by way of conclusion, it is necessary to make clear that we believe that knowledge is a vital part of life and success of people. Those who care enough to learn a little more every day become experts who can not only go far and make a lot of money, but who can influence and impact the lives of others in a positive way.

If somehow this book contributes to awaken your interest in Bitcoin and that leads you to learn more and more and become an expert, we will feel very proud of your progress because we know that you will have acquired tools that you will make available to other people so that they can also go far and be as successful as you. That is the interesting thing about this kind of phenomena and this kind of initiatives, that point towards a common benefit, towards the achievement of expectations that maybe other people would never believe because that is what this is all about, believing.

THE CREATORS OF BITCOIN BELIEVED, the creators of the altcoins that are already becoming established in the market also believed, and not only in themselves, but they also believed in other entrepreneurs, because to have developed an altcoin is because they first believed in

Bitcoin and realized that everything was a reality, and not a fraud as many others came to think at some point.

So, even if you are a small entrepreneur, even if you are perhaps an ordinary person who has not yet started your own business, all of us from the bottom of our hearts and from the most positive feelings that move these letters and make this book possible, we tell you that the time is now, that maybe you should not wait any longer because it may be too late. It is time to invest, and that investment does not have to be a large sum of money, in fact it does not have to be money as such. Thanks to all that we have discovered and put down in this book, thanks to all that we have read and written for you, we know that there are ways to acquire Bitcoins without investing a single cent, and then those Bitcoins can start to multiply by investing wisely, trading, scalping, and then even that money can multiply even more if we invest it in altcoins that can then increase their value in very high ways.

But none of this is possible if we do not invest first of all time and effort in learning, because the best trading is not done by people who do not know how to do it successfully, the same happens with scalping and many other strategies and techniques to multiply money. It's all about learning every day a little more and doing things in a positive way, because as we have already told you repeatedly, if all the knowledge leads you to success, that's fine, but if you know how to multiply not only your money but also your knowledge, and you know how to help other people to get as far as you, then it will be doubly successful and you can even conquer history and a whole market that is out there waiting for you.

So the question would be:

What are you waiting for? Have you already entered the sites to start earning Bitcoin without investing more than a few hours of your time? Have you already signed up to create your own free Bitcoin wallets or purses where you can have a space to store your Bitcoin without spending anything? Have you already spent time researching what are your best options once you have reached an amount, however small, of Bitcoin in which you can invest to multiply your earnings?

MAYBE YOU SHOULDN'T THINK about it too much, maybe it's just time to do it, to act, to stop pondering so much to turn your best thoughts and ideas into concrete facts. The knowledge is there. So are the opportunities. And we trust you, because we know that if you have taken the trouble and dared to get to this point and read this book and learn about all those details, it is because in one way or another you are already motivated, and that is undoubtedly the first step, the most important of all.

So don't think about it, don't hesitate any longer. Act, invest.

Because without a doubt, Bitcoin is the currency of the future, and the future is now.

11

MAKING PASSIVE INCOME WITH BITCOIN

As you may have noticed throughout the development of the book, there are currently several ways to generate money with cryptocurrencies, there are many opportunities. While there are some that are riskier (and depend on your ability) such as trading, DeFi platforms, etc, there are others that are more recommended and less risky, such as making Hodl of a cryptocurrency and wait for its price to rise, although this earning model is absolutely passive, as it is a long-term strategy, we have other strategies that can also help you generate passive income, as is the strategy that I will present below.

This strategy has existed for many years, is widely used by banks today, although in a higher percentage of profit, this generates interest with your assets.

In the world of cryptocurrencies this modality already exists and is led by one of the most reliable companies in the environment: BlockFi, which is backed by the Gemini exchange and people as recognized in the environment as Anthony Pompliano.

BlockFi allows us to transfer our funds to the platform and generate an annual interest that goes from 6% (for cryptocurrencies such as Bitcoin) or almost 10% with stablecoins (which are cryptocurrencies that are 1 to 1 with the dollar, such as USDT and USDC to name a few).

IF YOU ARE interested in this modality, you can open a BlockFi account at the following link and earn $250 of Bitcoin for free:

GET your BONUS on BlockFi here

IN CASE you are reading this book in the printed version you can scan the following QR code with your cell phone:

ABOUT THE AUTHOR

In order to conclude this book and thank you for taking the time to read it, I wanted to clarify a few things before finishing. Many people have tried dabbling in Cryptocurrencies, some with success others with moderate results, but all with results in the end, the important thing is that you keep in mind that the Cryptocurrency market is a very manipulated market, this is why I recommend that you always pay attention to the indicators that you can see in Trading View, see the signals it sends you, continue learning about trading, if you are interested you can dedicate yourself to them, but if you cannot dedicate yourself to do HODL (the meaning of this within the Cryptocurrencies is related to buy coins when there is an important drop (for example if Bitcoin is at $8000 and drops to $6500 that's where you buy and go buying as it goes down, never when it goes up, This is known as Dollar Cost Averaging is a very used strategy) and keep those coins for years until they double, triple or quadruple their value, as well did those early adopters who bought Bitcoin when it was worth $0.006 cents, did HODL for 10 years and when Bitcoin reached its historical maximum of $69,000 dollars they sold everything and became millionaires. But as always, choose the method you like the most and follow it.

Finally, I would like to ask you that if you found this book a great help, I would like to know your comments leaving me a review of this book so I can improve it and continue providing great books to you, my readers, whom I appreciate very much.

Without further ado, I bid you farewell
all the best